Clear Skies
&
Good fortune

Wings
of
Fortune

Wings
of
Fortune

E. A. Chevrette, Jr.

On the Cover:

An actual photo of the author being congratulated by his flight instructor at the completion of his first solo, September 20TH, 1959. The author was sixteen years old. The entire sequence was filmed by the authors father possessing a Kodak Super 8MM camera. The film was found in a closet almost fifty years later, and transferred to a DVD.

Edited by Katherine M. Jahn and Rebecca E. Blais

Book Design by Melissa Mykal Batalin

Printed by The Troy Book Makers in Troy, NY
on recycled, acid-free paper.
www.thetroybookmakers.com

ISBN: 1-933994-20-7
ISBN-13: 978-1-933994-20-8

Contents

Introduction

Throughout my life, I have yet to find a time period that is documented as closely as the hours and minutes a pilot spends in the air. This time, meticulously recorded in a logbook, is divided into columns and lines, each of which display the date, aircraft number, aircraft type and time in flight. This information is then categorized into daytime, nighttime, cross-country, solo, and instruction given and received. On the lines where the pilot has received instruction, you will find a signature with a number next to it. The signatures correspond to the flight instructors, a group of people I highly respect. In a column for remarks the pilot records the type of maneuvers performed and the weather conditions encountered.

These requirements are the basis for documenting sufficient flight-time experience in order to maintain proficiency and advancement to higher plateaus. To the uninitiated, these logbook entries look like a basic ledger. To the pilots, each line and column come to life.

There are other names that are not recorded in my logbooks, such as fellow pilots and mechanics, the latter to whom I owe as much credit to as the instructors. Through the acquiring of their combined knowledge I am able to write this story.

I consider myself fortunate to have been able to follow a field of endeavor by choice, in some cases even more so because I am able to sit and ponder these logbooks. Through the realization that as time passes our memories become less vivid, I have used a more reserved approach in writing this story. The real names of the characters have been changed, but the people places and events are real. This is a story about flying.

Chapter One

The airport is located at the bend in the Mohawk River; just northwest of where the Mohawk River joins the Hudson River. This location makes the airport easier to locate from the air than the ground. An old wing, sitting on its leading edge, at the beginning of the access road reads: Loudon Aircraft. (1)

In a parking lot at the bottom of a dusty road, stands an arched roofed, Quonset-hut structure with oversized doors at one end, typical of hangars in the 1940's and 1950's. Access to the block building attached to the south side of this structure is made through a green door, much in need of paint and door lock assembly. Once inside, I notice a counter with a green linoleum top. This stands in front of two desks, one of which supports a schedule book; the other, a roll top, plays host to numerous logbooks. Next to that stands an upright cabinet whose top drawer serves as a cash box.

Behind the desks, a piece of plywood is attached to the wall; cut and hinged together to make doors that cover the storage shelves. There is a phone booth to the left of the door, a Coke® machine selling soda at 10 cents a bottle, and an overstuffed couch that is perfect for napping or just sitting while engaging in hangar talk.

The three doors inside the office lead to the utility room, back maintenance shop, and of course, the hangar itself.

Upon entering the hangar, I notice the expansive height of the ceiling, which is even more pronounced by the suspended lights, whose bulbs no one volunteers to change. The three-sided hangar foundation stands two feet higher than the floor. The foundation supports large wood laminated beams, which form the sides and roof. At the east end of the structure stands the manually-operated wood hangar doors, whose tracks extend beyond the side of the building and require some serious maneuvering on windy days.

I spend some time surveying the local aircraft population, which range from fabric-covered machines to those whose shiny aluminum skins glisten in the sun. The aircraft are neatly parked on either side of the main taxiway, facing north and south. Some aircraft boast engine covers to keep small winged tenants from building nests inside the engine cowling. To keep the aircraft firmly in place when not in use, rope leads from each wing and tail to tie-downs set in the ground.

I listen intently to the sound of an engine as one aircraft becomes airborne off the north runway. I watch in awe as the aircraft departs to the north soon to become a mere dot against the blue summer sky. Seconds later, a small cloud of dust trails behind another airplane as it gently returns to Earth on the same grass and gravel runway. The summer breeze that brushes my face brings with it the smell of freshly mowed hay from an adjoining field. I find this fabulously intoxicating.

My fascination with airplanes had taken me through countless books, and into model building. Most of what I built were flying objects. My interest then worked into a passion, to the point that at sixteen years old I preferred to fly than to drive the family automobile. It is on an unexpected July afternoon this year when my dreams of actually flying become reality.

Carl Wilsey, a friend and local pilot, brings me to this airport, to introduce me to my flight instructor, Stan Ronowski.

Stan, who greets me with a handshake, laid-back personality, and big fatherly grin, stands just short of six feet tall. The gray hair around his temples gives contrast to his dark black hair. He is wearing black horn-rimmed glasses, the same color as his shoes and slacks. The hair on his barrel chest peers out over the open topped short sleeve shirt he is wearing. There is no leather jacket, goggles or the like; he is just a regular person that you would expect to see everyday in the street; hardly what I expected a pilot to look like.

I discover that he and other like-minded people shared something special as a group. It is hard to explain and even harder to resist, but on that day I, too become a member of the "group."

The aircraft we are to fly is a 1946 vintage, Piper J-3C Cub. Entrance is gained through a two-piece door, upper and lower half located on the right side of the airplane. Following a thorough preflight, which includes general inspection of the aircraft and checking proper quantities of gas and oil; I am directed to occupy the rear of the tandem-seating cabin, which includes dual controls. The interior is strictly functional, with walls of yellow fabric.

The seat belts are attached to the tubular frame next to the rudder cables running the full length of the machine. With my right hand, I hold the floor-mounted stick in front of me. Rudder pedals are mounted on either side of the instructor's seat. Just inside each pedal there is another, smaller pedal for the hydraulic brakes, which are operated by the heel of my foot and take some time getting used to. To my left, I notice the throttle. Below that a trim control. On my right is the carburetor heat control.

There are Plexiglas windows on both sides; the one on the left slides down inside the fuselage, and can be opened or held closed with a tightly set screw.

The rudimentary instrument panel supports the airspeed indicator, non-sensitive altimeter (2), compass, oil pressure and temperature gauges and tachometer. A small sign reads; "solo from rear seat only" (3).

The cabin heater control, also located on the instrument panel, requires me to reach over the front seat to operate. This action alone produces more heat than does the heater.

Another interesting gadget is the fuel gauge. Located in front of the windshield; a long metal rod bent over at the top keeps it from sliding down through the hole in the gas cap. The other end is attached to a shellac covered cork that floats inside the 12-gallon tank.

Stan pulls himself into the aircraft with the aid of the overhead structural tubing, and occupies the front seat. A tall thin, curly haired man approaches the aircraft; this is Don Mulligan, owner and operator of Loudon Aircraft.

"You guys all set?"

"All set." Stan replies.

I am now introduced to new vocabulary. Don asks for the throttle to be positioned, and after pulling the prop through twice, the command comes for: "brakes and contact."

Stan repeats the commands, and with one more pull the 65 horsepower engine comes to life. As we start to move, my instructions are to "taxi in "s" turn fashion" in order to see in front and on either side of the aircraft. As I taxi east from the open hangar doors, I see that the lone taxiway leads to the north-south runway, whose southend joins the east-west runway. Further to the east, in the distance, I can see Bald Mountain supporting a tall antenna, which can be seen long before the Hudson River is sighted.

When the plane enters the runway, old tires, painted white, lay flat on the ground to outline the perimeter of each runway and encircle the orange windsock located in the center of the field. Over the years, countless take- offs and landings have exposed the gravel that lies beneath the grass of each runway.

Turning into position for take-off, we begin accelerating under full power. I can feel the tail rise while the two main wheels stir up a little dust until all 1,200 pounds of people and machine became aerodynamically suspended in the invisible entity called air.

Cruising at 3,000 feet and 75 MPH, I am introduced to the basics of flight; straight and level, turns, climbs, glides, change of power settings, steep banked turns.

One of Stan's favorite maneuvers, uses a point on the horizon to continuously roll the aircraft 30 degrees to either side of level flight. I perform this coordination exercise for several miles while Stan chants,

"Rudder, rudder and stick." This he continues until my performance is acceptable.

I also get my first lesson in navigation. Mechanicville lies to the northeast; Saratoga to the north, and Albany to the south.

The highways, rivers and lakes seem so perfectly placed from this altitude that they resemble more of a model landscape than the real thing.

As the end of my third hour draws to a close, Stan comments as we walk from the airplane while simultaneously pulling on some nearby tall grass to chew on.

"You had a smile on your face for the last few lessons, that's good. Next time we will go upstairs and introduce you to stalls and spins."

My smile diminishes when I hear those words, "stalls and spins," because, while it seems exciting, it sounds intimidating even when spoken so casually. But the intimidation only drives my curiosity, so I start asking questions about these two maneuvers. Stan answers nonchalantly, "Just another maneuver." This is not the answer I was looking for, or so I thought. At the time Stan leaves me to fly with another student, I start asking more questions of the local pilot population.

One answer comes from Tex, pilot and aircraft owner. He is a man so thin, his clothes just seem to hang over his body. To this day I can't figure out why he was never called "slim". When answering questions he would always look at me through his thick glasses and think intently before responding. Today is no different. He would always reply, "Stan will show ya."

Don stands in the hangar doorway, hands on his hips, an L&M cigarette held between his teeth, which enabled him to smoke and smile at the same time.

"What's up there?" He knew there was something on my mind.

I start asking more questions.

"Yeah, the Cub's a good airplane to stall, spin too!" Don comments.

"What are they?" I ask.

"Oh, just call before you come out, you're gonna need a little room for those. Yup, Cub's a good machine for that."

For the next few days, my mind is in slight turmoil, not knowing what to expect from this word "stall", never mind the word "spin". However, my curiosity again takes over. I follow my instructions and call beforehand.

Stan greets me as I arrive at the airport. At first he has a serious look on his face as we walk to the airplane. This changes to a reassuring smile as he climbs into the front seat. To Stan, this is just another flight.

We climb around a few lingering clouds to 3,500 feet. Stan introduces me to my first stall. Stan pulls back on the stick and raises the nose until the airspeed has slowed sufficiently enough to cause the airplane to shake and buffet. The resulting loss of airspeed will no longer support flight. At the onset of the stall Stan recovers. It is not all that bad; my curiosity goes to work again and Stan has my full attention.

I learn that the emphasis is on lowering the nose, adding power and judicious use of the rudder to help keep the airplane under control. On my first attempt at recovery, I rapidly push the stick forward, pinning us against our belts. My rudder usage is slow, thus the airplane has a tendency to fall off on one wing. Practice continues. In slow flight I hold altitude and airspeed just above stall while the airplane buffets and shakes in defiance of such a maneuver. I continue to slow the airplane until the wing stalls - this I practice from level flight as well as during turns. After about 40 minutes, Stan announces, "I got it." Which means he is flying and not I.

At 3,500 feet, he explains how he enters a stall, and from there, using full left rudder he enters the spin. We will use the road intersection below and count three turns in half turn increments. In order to maintain 1300 rpm to keep engine temperature up, we do not use the throttle as a handhold.

"Now, stay on the controls and count with me."

At the onset of the stall, the aircraft falls off on the left wing, followed by the nose, right wing and my stomach. As Stan initiates the count, all I can see is the ground. The nose attitude of the airplane is now 60 degrees below the horizon. At this point, the window on the left side of the airplane starts rattling, as does the split door on the right due to the buffeting. The ground is spinning and the altimeter records our rapid loss of altitude. Recovery from the spin is initiated at two and one half turns, this followed by the recovery from the stall which culminates in our return to normal flight. Stan turns around to see my reaction. My expression had to be comical to witness; I am holding my nose to equalize the pressure in my ears and trying to smile and talk at the same time.

"Are you alright?"

"Wow, great!" I reply nasally but enthusiastically. With that Stan had to laugh.

It is now my turn. I regain the thousand feet we had lost and set up for my next spin. Stan sits with his feet flat on the floor, hands on the instrument panel and coaches me through. This one is all mine, Stan is not on the controls. I set the airplane up and enter the stall. I hold the stick as far back as it would go and apply full left rudder to enter the spin. The noises seem secondary on this one. Through the windshield I watch the road intersection below us turn like a huge four spoke wheel as Stan and I count the turns. What a thrill I am controlling the airplane in what I believe to be the greatest maneuver yet! Although I do not display the accuracy or finesse of my instructor, I recover from the spin and return to straight and level flight. Stan turns around, only to witness what is probably the largest smile ever recorded in history.

Later, as we walk away from the airplane, Stan gives me a big grin. I follow suit, and ask about future lessons. When I find out we will not be doing more spins I am actually disappointed. Instead, future lessons will be flying in the traffic pattern and learning take-offs and landings.

Successive lessons are spent learning to leave and return to the ground with some degree of precision and dignity, thus leaving the aircraft and its occupants in one piece. These words are easier said than performed. The object is to pick a point from the air and land on it.

My first contact with terra firma results in a resounding crunch. The main gear spreads apart on contact. In retaliation, the bungee cords; (shock absorbers) (4) pull the gear back into position and catapult us back into the air. Stan opens the throttle and we keep on going.

"Slow it down! Remember to slow down and stall the airplane just as it touches the runway!"

Second attempt: I held the airplane off the runway a little too long, and high. As the airplane starts sinking rapidly from underneath us, Stan wrestles the controls from me just as all three wheels collide with the runway.

Due to the acoustics in the Cub, hand signals and lip reading are as important to the lesson as is the actual flying. A good instructor always makes his point clear. Stan shakes his head, as he pushes his glasses back onto his nose and motions me on. I know exactly what he is thinking.

"Stop looking over the nose, look around it. Keep the airplane straight, get the stick back."

At one point, I would have given anything to go back upstairs and do more stalls and spins. Stan takes the punishment in stride, as does the airplane. At the end of one of these hourly sessions, those who witnessed the show make comments as we walk back to the hangar.

"Best bunch of controlled crashes we have ever seen."

"The birds have been sittin' on top of the hangar

watchin you guys."

"You guys can do more crash and goes in one hour than anybody we ever saw."

"Hey Stanley, I got the name of a good chiropractor for ya."

"Better get out the gravel truck to fill in all those holes." Stan looks at me. "We've all been there," and chuckles.

My introduction to simulated forced landings comes quite abruptly one afternoon. Shortly after take off, Stan reaches over and closes the throttle with his left had, at the same time turning around to look at me, "Where are you going to put it?" Knowing he will not get an answer, Stan proceeds with the demonstration. By the end of the session, I have learned to keep the nose down to maintain airspeed, pick my field, keep the wind direction in mind at all times, look for culverts, wires, trees, open areas, even roads, and catch my breath in that order. I question the presence of traffic and the use of roads.

"Your mother taught you to look before you cross the street, I'm going to teach to look before you land on it." This is done quite promptly.

Side slips to landing and go-arounds and crosswind corrections are also covered, with my performances improving to the point that my landings are more predictable – To everyone's delight. After I have eight hours logged, Stan informs me that in two weeks I will solo the airplane.

Next week's lesson goes well. After about 30 minutes, Stan has me pull the airplane over to the side of the runway. He opens the split door of the Cub and climbs out. Standing by the open door while fastening his seat belt to the seat, he issues instructions loud enough to be heard over the prop blast, "I want you to perform one take off and landing to a full stop and bring the airplane over here to me, where I will be standing with your parents. It will be lighter without me in it, thus it will get airborne faster and float a little longer near the ground. If you are not down AND rolling at the halfway point, go around and try again."

Flying solo today is the farthest thought from my mind; my only thoughts today are of flying the airplane with Stan. Little did I know, this is how it was planned. I taxi to the north end of the airport and take my position for my first solo take-off. I advanced the throttle, keeping the nose straight with the rudder and applying a little forward pressure on the stick to raise the tail. As the airplane accelerates, it reaches take-off airspeed a little sooner than before. Applying a little back pressure on the stick, I am airborne. The smoothness of the air compared to the runway is quite evident after lift-off. I look to my right to witness Stan's watchful eye. Stan is not sitting in front to correct any mistakes. This is for real.

At a predetermined spot on the downwind, I start my let down: watching airspeed, altitude and judging distance on the base leg. Then final approach. I keep the airplane in a steady glide until I fly over the tires that mark the end of the runway. Here, I close the throttle to idle, I can feel the airplane settle. Watching the left side of the nose, I keep pulling back on the stick, correcting direction with the rudder... I feel the wheels touch and hear the familiar rumble a Cub makes rolling over tufts of grass and gravel. Proceeding over to where Stan is standing, he greets me with a big grin and bone-crushing handshake. I complete a total of three take-offs and landings that day. I did it!

As we walk away from the airplane, Stan pulls on a length of tall grass to chew on, as we discuss the next step of my training. I follow suit and listen intently, relishing the sweet taste of the grass and the moment.

There are plenty of smiles, handshakes, and pats on the back. Let us not forget the bucket of cold water poured over my head; only the pilot gets wet, not his spirit. I am now officially a student pilot. This is the greatest adventure that a sixteen year old could ever experience, and I know it is not going to stop here.

E. A. Chevrette, Jr.

Chapter Two

Echo Charlie

It is a warm summer day as I arrive at the airport to find Don mowing the higher than normal grass around the hangar. This was not one of his favorite past times. Pushing the mower away, he turns toward me with a big Cheshire cat grin and one eye closed, "You still looking for a job?" I nod my head. "Yes". "Good."

"See what you can do with that mower," he says swatting at his head and laughing, " These mosquitoes are getting as big as the Cub."

"Here's the deal!" I am handed a small ledger book to keep track of my time. My forty-hour workweek will be reimbursed at a rate of $1.00 per hour, in trade for flying time. And so our business deal begins.

After restarting the mower, we both question how the mosquitoes can stand all the smoke. Mowing, however, is not the only part of my indoctrination into the real business of flying.

Sweeping the office and hangar floors, washing airplanes, and keeping track of the gasoline each airplane consumed daily were all part of my tasks. Twice a week I would hitch the home made trailer to the back of Don's old Chevy to transport the empty oil cans and trash to a dump just to the east of the north-south runway. This is located on site, making a driver's license unnecessary.

Many airplanes still require hand propping. Strict instructions from Don minimized the hazard. I even learn how to prop the Cubs from behind the propeller. This became useful when performing the morning run-up on each Cub by myself. I learn how to clean Plexiglas windshields with a hard to remove polish; and underbellies with gasoline. Tapping an engine gauge with one's finger is a good remedy for the occasional sticky indicator needle.

Installing new tie downs for the airplanes is an interesting process because each, about four feet high, has an eyelet at the top and a screw anchor on the bottom end. Inserting a long metal bar at the top and walking in continuous circles until installation is complete brings much attention and little assistance. Comments made by the local pilot population as they walk by are hardly original.

Adding 100-octane aviation gas to our inventory requires the installation of another underground tank. My job, on a hot summer afternoon, is to cover the tank with tar. When I am through; the only item not covered with tar is the top of my right shoe! I remind myself, "It's all part of the business." Fortunately, installing underground tanks is not an every day occurrence.

My responsibilities soon include answering the phones, scheduling flights and servicing transient aircraft. Conversations with these pilots ranged from talking about the airplanes, to the weather, to the weathervane located in the next field just north of the airport. I soon learn that the quiet soft-spoken pilots have more interesting information, friendlier personalities and as a whole seem to be more capable aviators than I imagine.

Their occasional loud counterparts, however, seemed more interested in attracting attention; one in particular of whom I take great pleasure informing that his airport of intended landing, Albany, is another five miles to the southwest.

Providing charter flights is as common to the business as flight instruction. Kenney Derringer, probably one of the youngest flight instructors in the area, employed full time, is as equally engaged as Don.

Arriving for work one morning, I noticed the airport to be unusually quiet. Masking tape is used to fasten a note on the door leading to the hangar, informing me that both men are flying charter, and that I would be alone for most of the day. This intrigues me, for it will be the first time, save for the actual flying that I will be in charge of the operation. This ignites my determination to do well.

Later in the morning, while I direct an airplane to a parking space at the end of the taxiway, I inquire of the pilot about the unusual blue and white color scheme on his Cub (as opposed to the standard yellow on most Cubs). To this he replies rather proudly; " these are my favorite colors", and requests directions to a phone and a cold drink. He informs me he is delivering this airplane to its new owner, and another aircraft, a similarly painted Cessna 140, flown by one of his students, will arrive shortly for his return flight home. Over a cold Coke we discover we have mutual interests. What we do not know, however, is that the rest of our day will be far from routine.

The windsock indicates wind out of the west-northwest; thus the north is the preferred runway today. After circling overhead, the pilot makes his first approach for the south runway, thus attempting a crosswind downwind landing. His first attempt is too high, and too fast. The second attempt finds us standing alongside the runway, waiving our arms in a gesture to gain his attention and land the opposite direction. There is yet another go-around. His third attempt in the same direction results in using two thirds of the runway before his first bounce. On the third bounce the airplane is just short of the hedgerow that marks the end of the south runway. At this point the pilot locks the brakes, causing the Cessna to nose over as it passes through the hedgerow, making a sound like a huge drum as the airplane finally comes to a rest upside down.

Utilizing the skills I learned in track, I start running toward the hedgerow. I have no idea what I am going to do when I arrive at the scene. Fortunately for me, Don had just landed the Cessna 170B on the west runway, just in time catch the show.

We approach the hedgerow where the Cessna was hiding just in time to see the pilot crawl out of the inverted cockpit. Don and I climb around the end of the hedgerow to assist and question his physical well-being. The odor of gasoline attracts our attention more so than does his answer. The pilot, slightly shaken, attempts to light a cigarette. With that, we start a retreat while Don gives the best piece of advice;

"I would not do that if I were you!"

With that said, our pilot friend returns the cigarettes

to his pocket.

Directing his comment to the pilot, Don inquires if all the switches and gas valves are turned off. The student is still speechless. Don turns to me; "Eddie, take a look inside." I carefully climb into the inverted cockpit. My familiarities with two similar airplanes based here prove useful to me as I start my investigation. Lying on my back on the ceiling I locate the master switch, gas valve and ignition switch and render each to the "off" position. Crawling back out of the airplane, I cannot imagine what it would be like to experience what just happened from inside the airplane. I make a mental note never to find out.

While Don is talking to the student and his instructor, I notice if the airplane were allowed to roll though the hedgerow, there would have been plenty of room to stop in the adjacent field, probably with negligible damage to the aircraft. By late afternoon, the aircraft is retrieved (5) and secured for disassembly and future transport to home base. At this point Don makes another observation,

"That used to be a perfectly good airplane. See what happens when one does not think?"

This is not the last time I will hear words of wisdom.

Later that day, just before closing, Don has his big Cheshire cat grin on his face, which is followed by a hearty laugh, "I guess you had one hellava first day as an airport operator!"

Richard Waterman, an aircraft mechanic, pilot and local aircraft owner, joins in the laughter. He then forges a serious look, grasps his oversized glasses in thumb and forefinger, which is usually done prior to his speaking;

"I understand you have a slightly used Cessna 140 you might sell cheap." This rekindles the laughter. He has a very down to earth sense of humor, appreciated by all who know him. Both men have been associates and friends for years, and although they have different personalities, both are of similar thought. My education on the ground and in the air complement each other.

After a few hours spent with Stan on windy days, more solo time on the better ones, I am informed it is now time to start cross-country flying.

I purchase my first aeronautical chart, an Albany sectional for twenty-five cents. On the back of the chart is a listing of all the airports depicted and a brief description of each. I learn how to locate an airport using longitude and latitude, and with the aid of a protractor, plot a course from one airport to another. My E6B computer is basically a slide rule formed in a circle with a movable grid for computing wind corrections and ground speed. With this information I compute the ETA and total fuel consumption on what is to be my first cross-country flight, southeast to Great Barrington, Massachusetts.

On this initial cross-country flight I learn two types of navigation; One by a predetermined compass course; referred to as dead reckoning, the second, referencing the chart for checkpoints confirming my location, is called pilotage.

In flight, I notice that while cities and towns are easily found, some of the small villages that appear as circles depicted on the chart are more challenging. One such location is Austerlitz, New York; which I find after Stan places the Cub on its left wing and points toward a dozen buildings. Hills and mountains are shown on the chart in varying degrees of color and shapes with the lighter colors indicating higher terrain. Matching colors and shapes to the real elevations requires good observation, which I learn as we approach Great Barrington. Passing the ridge, I continue toward the airport. Circling to the left I see the north-south grass runway, and the main east west, hard surfaced runway; the latter is our choice for landing.

Making my first approach to a strange airport is exciting. This is also my first landing on a hard surfaced runway. Crossing the threshold of the runway, I close the throttle and wait in anticipation for the "squeal" as both balloon tires touch the macadam surface.

As we deplane on a hard surfaced ramp, I am in awe, looking at all the airplanes located here, especially the new ones located by the operations building and the twin-engine aircraft located in the separate hangar. Inside the operations building, a large model of an F4U Corsair fighter hung from the ceiling. In a brief conversation, the operator casually informs me he used to fly a Corsair. Politely, Stan reminds me we have two more legs to cover on our flight. I make a mental note to return some day and finish my conversation.

At the end of the taxiway just prior to our takeoff, we are the recipients of a casual wave as a station wagon passes by on the county road adjacent to the runway threshold.

Leaving Great Barrington and heading west, I am to choose a heading in reference to the mountains. This will allow me to climb on course with few deviations due to the higher terrain. We are headed for Germantown, New York, landing at Webber Field, located on the Hudson.

Finding this airport is little more challenging; for it blended well into the countryside. Weber Field hosts two grass runways; one approximately twelve hundred feet long; the other is considerably shorter. There is nothing in the way of creature comforts, just a hangar in much need of attention with matching office. Not exactly the place one would write home about, however, a good place for navigational practice and a short field landing.

Our return trip takes us north, up the Hudson Valley. I think this will be easy, and decide to sit back and enjoy the ride. Stan has other ideas.

"Not all days are going to be this easy to navigate." He has me pick out every railroad, highway, power line, and island in the river, including tributaries that feed the river.

"Get into the habit of knowing where you are every minute. Navigate close to the airplane."

After our landing, Stan informs me the next trip will be to Rutland, Vermont; Glens Falls, New York and back home. I am to preplan the entire flight;

I will deal with higher mountains, larger airports, and for the first time, use the radio for navigation. From the bottom drawer of the filling cabinet, I remove the radio, a Motorola Airboy. (6)

Walking out to the airplane with my chart, E6B

computer, radio, about the size of a lunch box, two headsets and headset adapter, there are a few comments made. According to Tex, all Lindbergh had was a pencil. Ted Lorn, a tall lean quiet man, who reminds me of Ichabod Crane, asks where I am going to put all that stuff; "By the way. Don't get on the wrong river." To this a few pilots chuckle, one of them being Stan as he follows me to the airplane. I am given another pleasant surprise. I will fly this trip in the front seat, affording me a much better view of the countryside.

On the way to Rutland, the mountainous terrain starts at a small town called Shushan. Here, without assistance, I pick out a small airport at the base of the mountain, the home of a small hangar and one airplane. I am so engrossed while navigating in the valley between the striking green mountains I am oblivious to loss of RPM; the first sign of carburetor ice. After applying heat, the problem is remedied. I am learning that navigation is only part of each trip.

Just south of the city of Rutland, Stan points out the airport. Overhead, I look at a paved runway over a mile long. Mountains to the east and north require a non-standard right hand traffic pattern for the south runway. This is another first.

Departing Rutland, climbing in circles to clear the mountains, we head southwest toward Glens Falls. The view of the Hudson Valley is very distracting requiring a concerted effort on my part to concentrate on navigating and not sightseeing.

Before departing Glens Falls, Stan briefs me on the

radio. We will navigate using the low frequency Albany Radio range. Specifically, the north leg, southbound. This is one of four legs, each transmitted through corresponding towers located just north of the Albany Airport. Between each leg are quadrants, alternating A and N, identified by Morse code for each letter. With the aid of our headsets, we listen to the Morse code identifier for Albany and the code for each quadrant. A steady hum between each Morse code identifier is the signal we are on course.

The trip back to Loudon takes us down the Hudson Valley, with the river on our left and the feet of the Adirondacks to the right. Using the audio cues and pilotage, we navigate toward the range station, periodically lowering the volume as the distance to the station diminishes. Upon approaching the station there is sudden increase in volume, then silence; hence the cone of silence, which is directly over the range station.

After returning home, I notice a constant ringing in my ears. For the next half hour, everyone I talk to sounded like Donald Duck. Putting my fingers in my ears in an attempt to stop the ringing does not work. I learn that getting used to the side affects of a headset is yet another first. Later, as Stan endorses my logbook, he informs me that when I receive my restricted radio operator's permit we will take a trip to Albany. I will then be exposed to communicating with the tower and executing clearances.

When he is through, he comments in a voice for all to hear;

"Look at this; we are getting some flying time in our logbook." while holding it open for all to see.

"Don't forget to study the phonetic alphabet in the Airman's Guide before we go to Albany."

The following week I receive my permit. I feel as though I have hit the big time, as I tell all the pilots I will be flying into a controlled airport. Don, Stan, Ted, Tex and a few more pilots sitting in the office affectionately query my knowledge of the phonetic alphabet.

"Do you know what the A is?"

"Yes; Alpha."

"What about the S?"

"Ahh that is Sierra."

"If you're thirsty, what does the W stand for?"

"Whiskey."

This goes on for a few minutes until Stan looks at me and asks, "Your initials are EC; what do they stand for?"

I look at him quizzically. Then answer; " Echo Charlie." (7)

And so I am christened with a new nickname.

After settling down in the Cub, each of us with a headset, wires and now a microphone, it is a wonder there is room to turn our heads.

Listening to the response of my first attempt at contacting the tower is as eye opening as the speed of the Convair that had just passed us on the right, headed for the same runway. The rapid response is filled with words and phrases I have never heard, add to the fact our reception on this small radio left much to be desired. The result; confusion.

Stan turns around to give me some instructions, when another similar airplane proceeds to follow the first. Things are getting a little interesting; Stan is helping me understand the clearance from the control tower, I am holding the microphone with the same hand I need to fly the airplane with, and now we approach the threshold of the runway. Stan makes a life saving announcement; "I got it." Stan then applies full power and flies the airplane down the runway to the first intersection, lands and promptly clears the main runway, in what seems like one maneuver. Once cleared of the active runway, Stan turns us around just in time to see a Lockheed Constellation touch down on the same runway we had just vacated, with a landing speed much faster than our cruising air speed. Stan announces that one had to be very careful when mixing different types of aircraft.

" Listen to the tower, keep your head on a swivel. Things happen a little quicker here."

We proceed with more take offs and landings that require more concentration listening to the phraseology, and more work flying the airplane within clearance limits given by the tower. I am sure the voice of the pilots and controllers sound a lot larger than does the one coming from this Cub. About one hour later, slightly fatigued, but much wiser and still in good spirits, we depart for home. I look out the side window toward Albany Airport with its three large runways and one thought stayed in my head. I want to go back.

The arrival of fall brings with it great scenery and new regulations. Pilots are routinely flying longer distances. The basic lack of knowledge by non-instrument rated pilots to fly an airplane solely by instruments is becoming a growing concern. Such a pilot can find himself in a condition where flying the airplane with little or no outside references is a very dangerous situation. Pushing one's luck can be disastrous. To help remedy this situation, all non-instrument rated pilots are now required to perform at least basic instrument maneuvers under simulated conditions, including basic navigation and recovery from unusual attitudes.

Many of the airplanes on the field have gyroscopic instruments for attitude and direction. The Cubs did not. In order to comply with even the basic instruments, sensitive altimeter and turn and slip indicator are installed in the Cub. (8) Once the installation is complete, I can hardly wait to tell Stan and try my hand at instrument flying. After a brief discussion, Stan makes the point that the airplane still flies the same; only my point of reference is changed; I will rely solely on the instruments.

Once again, I am in the front seat of the Cub, allowing me an unobstructed view of the instrument panel. After take-off, I put the "hood" on my head. This is like a cap with a long beak and is designed to restrict one's vision to the instrument panel. Whoever designed this contraption had to be sadistic, for it is uncomfortable and rarely stays in one position. Whenever I get into a maneuver that had any G forces, or turbulence, it would fall down in front of my face just when I needed to see the instrument panel.

Once airborne, Stan instructs me on the basic maneuvers, which helps with instrument familiarization. My first reaction is to feel the airplane. This is wrong; I need to first read the instruments. Secondly, overreacting to every movement of the instruments with a corresponding control movement causes over controlling and only adds to the work of instrument flying. Every so often, I am inclined to try and peek from under the hood to see what the ground looks like. This sneak peek is followed by a tap on the shoulder and the command; "No Peeking!"

As the needle swings back and forth I learn to average the readings. I learn to crosscheck with other instruments, and ultimately I am accomplishing the basic maneuvers, including climbs, glides and slow flight with reasonable proficiency. I am then taken to the next plateau.

A command comes from Stan to look at my lap. At this point, the aircraft is placed into an unusual attitude. On his command I respond hesitantly, "Ok you got it." I scan the instrument panel, making a fast assessment of the maneuver, then recover to level flight. There is a stall recovery, then the opposite. The aircraft is in a banked, steep nose down spiral at a higher than normal airspeed. Stan sets up another maneuver. I decide one more time to take a quick look outside to satisfy my curiosity. I know Stan must have seen my head move, for suddenly the maneuver becomes more abrupt. I then realize I have never seen the ground like this before and immediately look back at my lap. I can almost see Stan smiling in the backseat.

During the final maneuver, I can feel Stan slow the airplane down. The airplane shudders for a moment, and then the floor drops out from underneath me.

"Put your hands and feet on the controls," Stan commands. I comply.

"Now look at the instrument panel and tell me what the airplane is doing."

The stick is fully back and the rudder as far left as it can go. "This has got to be a spin," I say to myself. I look at the instrument panel and notice the airspeed indicates a stall condition, the compass is spinning one direction then the other, and the altimeter is unwinding.

"That is what a spin looks like on the gauges. Now recover." Stan directs.

My mind is working feverishly; I know how to spin an airplane and recover using outside references, and I know how sensitive these instruments are to control pressures. But now I must put the two together and recover to a more stable flight attitude. It is time to go to work.

I start my initial recovery and apply opposite rudder to counteract the rotation, which takes a half turn to stop. I must be careful not to overact - once rotation is stopped I can concentrate on recovery from the stall. The compass is unreadable and useless until I reach level flight. The ball has moved to the left side of the casing and as the rotation ceases, the needle moves to the right side of the instrument. This should mean that rotation has all but stopped. With this accomplished, I neutralize the rudder as the airspeed returns faster than I expect due to the nose down attitude. The physical sensations I am experiencing in this maneuver are telling me to fly the airplane entirely differently than the information I am reading on the instrument panel. I am actually experiencing vertigo.

I am doing my best to ignore my feelings and put my complete concentration and trust in the instrument panel. This is real work, however I stick with it and manage a recovery. Then Stan removes the hood from my head; "Let's go home", as a big grin occupies his face.

Looking at the instrument panel I realize that I am dealing with a panel of consultants; all must be dealt with before arriving at any conclusion. I remove a slight trace of perspiration and brush the hair from my forehead. I check the position of each wing tip and that of the nose. We are in trimmed level flight, a condition that requires little, if any control adjustments. The instruments on the panel concur this with a look of serenity, even though a few seconds ago, their faces told a different story. I quietly enjoy the tranquility of the short flight home with a greater respect for airplanes and those who fly them.

The inevitable winter follows. Preflight requires more care due to snow, ice and cold. Salamander type heaters are necessary for engine preheating. Due to the Cubs inadequate cabin heating system, long underwear and warm jackets and a strong desire to fly are standard wintertime operating procedures. Some days are so cold, the engine tachometer cable actually snaps in flight. Wind only added to the bitterness of the cold.

On one cold winter day, Don takes me to the back of the hangar where we dust off a pair of aluminum skis.

"There ya go, this'll take some of the bite out of 'ole man winter", Don said.

We proceed to remove the wheels from the Cub and replace them with the skis. There are two bungee cords, one for the toe and the other for the heel of each ski. These are attached to the bottom of the airplane to keep each ski in the proper landing position while in flight.

After the installation is complete, to keep the skis from freezing to the ground when the airplane is not in use, we place a flat piece of wood under each ski. The airplane looks neat sitting there. Stan remarks, "Jump in!" Without hesitation, I comply.

Taxiing is a little different because you have no brakes. This requires giving yourself extra room. When turning, you literally have to blast the tail around with power to accomplish a turn. If you find yourself near other airplanes on the ramp, it is best to shut down and walk the airplane into position.

Mag check and carb heat check are done on the run. With the absence of the balloon tires to absorb some of the shock, the take-off and landing roll are a little stiffer than normal. After a few touch and go landings, Stan taxis over to the unplowed snow in the field between the two runways. As the aircraft accelerates, I glance down at the ski slicing through the virgin snow and at times almost disappears as we reach take off speed.

On the final approach, I used the marks left by

our own skis to reference the landing. We keep this up, making more tracks with little evidence of where they originated from or departed to. When turning in the powdered snow, the propeller blast creates a huge white cloud as if to camouflage the airplane from view. After about an hour, Stan climbs out of the airplane.

"Go do some on your own, just watch for traffic on the north-south runway."

Winter flying, at least for me, has taken on a new dimension; besides, this looks great in my logbook! (9)

Chapter Three

Of Fabric and Paper

During an annual inspection on one of the Cubs, the outer layer of fabric that covers the airplane failed the punch rest. (10) The entire aircraft is disassembled and the sections are rendered to the shop for the first step in the recovering process. After the aircraft sections are placed in the shop, I inquire as to the procedure for removing the old fabric. With a smile on his face, Don hands me a knife, "Here, this and a little imagination will do the trick."

I look at the knife inquisitively, "Do I cut it off?" I asked.

"That's right, go to it!"

I can hardly believe it; this is like having a bucket of bricks and permission to throw them through a plate glass window. Sometime later, after I have removed the fabric from most of the fuselage, Don reenters the shop. Here I stand, oversized coveralls, face covered in dirt, with sheets of old fabric piled up to my knees. Don chuckles, as he directs me to a spot outside where I can proceed with the disposal. Handing me a book of matches he says, "Here, there are two matches inside the cover. I want one of them to light my cigarette."

Within seconds of igniting one piece of fabric, a fire producing thick black smoke is billowing into the air. Within minutes the entire pile of old fabric is diminished to ashes. As I stand there watching the fire in awe, Don, with his arms folded comments, "Good reason not to smoke in a fabric covered airplane!"

The tubular frame is sanded to bare metal, inspected for cracks and corrosion, repaired if necessary, then painted with a zinc chromate primer. This second step in the recovery process also includes inspecting and making any necessary repairs to the wing sections, control surfaces and control cables.

The third step: fabric is purchased in rolls and sewn together to make sleeves to fit the fuselage, wing and tail sections. When available, presewn sleeves can save the mechanic considerable time (11). Fabric on each wing panel requires stitching the material to each wing rib with a wax coated fiber material. This is knotted at the top of the wing rib to permanently conform the fabric to the shape of the wing. The fabric is treated with layers of butyrate dope for protection and rigidity; feelings of euphoria can result from exposure to the fumes for any length of time.

Audiences are not uncommon in the shop while work is in progress; a project such as this will last most of the winter, thus giving the pilot population a reason to gather at the airport even on bad weather days. Conversations concerning the structure of the airplane and how it appears without its cloth covering soon change to; flying, politics, weather, and the economy, and invariably lead to the subject of women. I did not realize aviation was such a well-rounded education.

Coincidently, the engine is close to its overhaul time, and is removed and placed on a wooden workbench, one end of which acts as a jig for just this purpose. I am to work with Richard Ellington; mechanic and long time friend of Don Mulligan. He is a slender, quiet, soft-spoken man who always wears a friendly smile, and refers to me as Slick.

After each individual engine part is removed, I assist by washing them in a very powerful solvent contained in a fabricated 55-gallon drum. Richard's insistence for proper apparel, coveralls, gloves and eyewear, make me look more like a refugee than a mechanic's helper.

Under Richards's guidance, I am experiencing hands on, the overhaul and reassembly of each individual part and its relationship to the proper operation of the engine. His instructions conclude with the application of spar varnish to the wooden propeller; this is accomplished literally by hand, without the aid of a brush.

Despite all of this work, the greatest thrill is yet to come; the day I actually fly this airplane.

Late one winter afternoon, with forecasts of an impending nor'easter, all efforts are directed toward packing five airplanes into a hangar normally intended for three. The first Cub is placed nose first toward the back wall. There, three of us lift up the tail over our heads to allow the nose of the airplane to rest on a five-gallon paint bucket placed on the hangar floor with a seat cushion atop. The second Cub is parked similarly behind the first. The Cessna 170, 172 and the Tri-Pacer are jockeyed into position, running main wheels up on wood planks allows the wings to overlap: this efficient utilization of floor space will allow enough room to close the large hangar doors.

After retiring to the office, Stan approaches me with the idea that we take a winter cross-country in the Tri-Pacer to Canastota, New York. We will include Nellis field westbound and Cooperstown on the return leg. For me this is flying in style- a four place airplane, two cabin heaters, electric system with built in radios, upholstered interior, tricycle landing gear, a control wheel instead of a stick, and 36 gallons of gas; enough to make the entire trip without refueling. I diligently plan my trip and hope for better weather.

The day finally arrives. As Stan and I climb into the front seats, my father occupies the rear. Heading west past Schenectady along the Mohawk River Valley, the ground slips past at a speed almost twice what I am accustomed to. And landmarks covered with a fresh blanket of snow create a challenge to navigation.

East of Canajoharie is a narrow pass in the Mohawk River valley, its venturi effect increases the speed of the already brisk west wind evidenced by the blowing and drifting of snow on the downwind side. Checking my chart, I notice that there is a road heading south, another heading west, which should pass adjacent to Nellis field. Diligently I follow this road until I am above the half plowed east west runway. Below, a lone snowplow slowly makes its way through the deep snow. To the north of the runway and behind the snow covered "T" hangars is a stately looking inoperative beacon, with attached windsock showing a brisk west wind. We decide to fly over Nellis field and continue to our destination.

Tuning the radio to the Utica VOR, I am instructed on the basics of VOR navigation. After station passage, I use the radio and with the aid of my chart follow a railroad track that passes adjacent to the airport. Once overhead I note the single taxiway toward the west end of the east west runway, both appear to be recently cleared of snow with the windsock indicating a west wind.

Stan announces our arrival over the Unicom frequency as I proceed to take a position in the traffic pattern. We know the snow banks around the runway are high, and this being my first landing in the Tri-Pacer, I welcome Stan's assistance. After touchdown, the snow banks prove to be considerably higher than the airplane, and adds a challenge to finding the taxiway. The only parking space available on the ramp is next to one of the snow throwers used to clear the runway. This is a huge machine that dwarfs our airplane.

After a brief break, we depart for Cooperstown, Westville, and once overhead, I discover an airport buried in snow. Stan challenges my navigation and asks me to prove my location. By using several landmarks as reference, the challenge is met. The final leg to Albany is accomplished solely under simulated instrument conditions, and radio navigation. Since we have a full panel of gyro instruments, this proves quite a treat.

After the flight, Stan signs my solo cross-country endorsement on my Student Pilot Certificate, then proceeds to fill out my logbook. Stan comments; "Look

at this, the flight time in the Tri-Pacer completes another
page in your logbook." This is cause for a student to strut
momentarily while holding his logbook for all to see.
By comparison, my instructor, after making entries in
a logbook four times larger than mine, quietly places it
back in the drawer.

Spring arrives, turning the airport into one big mud
hole. Wood planks, full sheets of plywood and a lot of
muscle are used to get the machines to one of the very
few dry spots on the airport. In some cases, we would
work for hours just to get a few minutes in the air.

With early summer, comes longer days and better flying weather. Don and I agree it is time for me to complete
the solo cross-country flight requirements and the Cub will
be a good airplane to use. I inquire as to the feasibility of
flying the later model Cub from the front seat. Don replies
with an interesting answer; "In your travels around the
airport, get an old Cub tire and inner tuber, fill them with
rocks and buckle them into the rear seat for ballast, you'll
be alright." With a little effort, determination and a slight
interest in anthropology, it is done.

Glens Falls, New York, Bennington, Vermont, and
Great Barrington are just a few airports I visit in my
travels. On a return trip from Great Barrington, I stop at
Germantown Airport; here I successfully make a short

field landing on my first approach. Walking away from the airplane, I am greeted by the operator, dressed in old coveralls and smoking what is left of his cigar, "What can I do fer ya young fella?"

Handing him my logbook and pen I ask for his signature. (12) With that he comments," I don't get to sign many of these, ya see, most pilots give up after three approaches and go someplace else."

On the return flight up the Hudson Valley, I admire the vastness of the Catskill Mountains to the west and make a mental note to someday locate the airports near Freehold and Catskill, both depicted on my chart. Just south of Albany, I then take a heading that I have calculated will bring me over my house. The calculation soon proves accurate - approaching overhead at 2000 feet I slide the window open. From this altitude, if I yell loud enough, I know I will be heard on the ground, thus I proceed to inform the entire neighborhood that I will be landing at 5 pm. This insures me a ride home and a seat at the dinner table.

The longest cross-country flight will be the same one flown the previous winter with Stan in the Tri-Pacer, with a few exceptions; One, I will fly solo; two, my airspeed will be slightly more than half, and three, I will not have a radio. Equipped with one Albany Sectional, one Cub with twelve gallons of gas, one E6B calculator and a tire full of rocks as my rear seat passenger, I am on my way to my first airport, Nellis Field.

Westbound at 3,000 feet against a constant headwind, with airspeed around 75 miles per hour, getting past thruway traffic below is interesting. I have been watching a Greyhound Bus disappear and reappear under my right tire for the last twenty miles; flying a straight line eventually proves the Cub the victor. Leaving the river valley to the north I proceed to Nellis Field. The paved east west runway is easily recognized by the slight bend in the middle. Using my airport knowledge, I know I have plenty of room to land and clear the mowing in progress on the north side of the runway located at midfield. The landing is successful.

Crawling out of the Cub onto freshly mowed grass, I hear a voice ask, "Where ya from?"

"Loudon Airport. Took about 50 minutes," I respond.

"I've done a little better, when I didn't chase traffic," he remarks with a grin. We retire to the luncheon shack; where, after a brief conversation and some refreshment; I pay for my milk a donut and gas, and then crawl back into the Cub. Departing, I give the customary wave.

Westbound south of Utica, the terrain becomes much flatter. Smaller airfields are more numerous with some actually carved out of cornfields. Following two great checkpoints, a double track railroad, paralleled by a highway, I am overhead Canastota one hour after departing Nellis. Today, the airport seems much friendlier without snow.

The closest parking area places me a good distance from the pumps, where a man and small boy are standing near the fence watching the airplanes. When I ask for his signature in my logbook he flatly refuses; "I don't sign anything," he says as he turns and walks away. This I find irritating.

Behind me I heard another voice; "You need gas?" I look over at this figure in coveralls, leaning against the gas pumps while wiping his hands with a rag, "Yes!"

"Well bring her over." Picking up the tail of the Cub by the rear handle and pointing it in the desired direction, I proceed to walk the airplane to the gas pumps, and remove the gas cap. (13)

"You're kinda self sufficient there young fella. When I top her off, I'll sign that logbook for ya. By the way, don't let them bystanders bother ya, they're all a pain in the neck anyway. See ya flyin from the front seat, what's in the back?" The entire conversation is neatly choreographed around his tobacco chewing ritual.

"One tire full of rocks for weight," I reply.

With a huge grin, he looks at me, and comments, "Plexiglas cleaner is next to the Coke machine. After you wet your whistle you can get that bug juice off yer windshield." With a big smile on my face I thank him.

Departing Canastota, I fly a southeasterly heading and tend to the business of navigating. About an hour later, after flying over rolling hills and farmland I arrive at Cooperstown Westville airport, on the southern tip of Otsego Lake. After landing, I taxi onto what appears to be a gravel parking area and shut down the airplane next to an old shack.

The wind that blows dust across the ramp lazily opens and closes the shack door against the jam. I investigate the adjacent hangar that houses an old tractor and some airplane parts, all-foreign to me. Judging the dust collection on the old weather beaten gas pump, it has seen better days. It is also obvious that I am the only soul on the field, even my airplane N92210, looks homesick - this is obviously a poor choice of airports.

The last leg home is little more than an hour, and for all practical purposes, my fuel if half gone. I look at my chart for an alternate landing site- Cooperstown Airport, just northwest of the town will solve this problem.

Next problem: I have started these Cubs alone at home: however, each one was tied down. But this is not the case here. I try to think of a way to minimize the possibility of the airplane getting away from me after propping the engine. If I close the fuel valve, it will limit the amount of fuel available to the engine, preventing the airplane from traveling too far before the engine stops. Although I have never actually tried this before, it sounds good in thought.

I close the throttle and place the fuel valve in the off position, magneto switch on. Standing behind the prop I pull it through and the engine starts on the first try, whereby I neatly slide back into the front seat, take a deep breath and prepare for my next stop.

My arrival at Cooperstown brings more interesting news: The airport I had just left is operated only on a part time basis, and then the operator at Cooperstown advises me he has no gas. After a short discussion, I am over Otsego Lake headed for Nellis Airport. There, I discuss my adventures with the instructor I had conversed with earlier that day. With a big smile on his face, he directs me to the phone booth inside the luncheon shack. I refuel and head for home.

There is a certain comfortable feeling that accompanies the arrival of familiar territory after a long trip. Pondering my flying experience that day, given the scarcity of information regarding many of these airports, I relied on my experience at Loudon Airport, which literally saved the day. With the Private Pilot written exam behind me, I look forward to preparation for my flight test.

A few days later, Don, Kenney and I are discussing my flight check while finishing a one hundred hour inspection on one of the Cubs. Don is sitting in the rear seat, when I jokingly ask if the taxiway is long enough for a take off. He looks at Ken, then me,

"Check to see if there is any traffic in the pattern." The pattern is empty. Power is applied, at first the airplane is held in place with brakes, after release a take off is commenced. Don is airborne as he crosses the runway and heads toward the southeast where the high grass partially hides the west runway from our viewpoint. As he banks, it looks as though the right wing tip and landing gear are just brushing the high grass. Here, we are treated to a rare look at the top side of the airplane while in flight. Leveling out, below tree-top level, he heads for the trees that skirt the far south end of the airport. There he proceeds to turn to the left in another similar maneuver.

Beyond the airport boundary to the east there is a

drop-off toward the Cohoe's Falls. It is there the aerial ballet continues. With the nose pointed down, he disappears, only to reappear in a nose high attitude as the sun glistens off the top of the wings highlighting his aerial ballet. This is followed by another turn to the north, making him barely visible as he drops down behind the trees where he obviously picks up speed. Pulling up to the vertical with another quick 180-degree turn only to disappear behind the trees again. He reappears just south of the east west runway completing a 270-degree turn to realign the airplane with the runway. He then side slips the airplane from left to right side until one wheel then the other produce a slight puff of dust as the airplane touches down on the dry runway. He adds just enough power to taxi all the way back to the pumps, never allowing the tail wheel to touch the ground until the airplane is almost stopped. I stand in absolute awe and realize that this is what the word "good" looks like in flight; a word worth achieving.

Stan is on a temporary leave of absence, thus Dave Walbridge, the newest member of our staff, is to be my instructor. Dave is a very quiet spoken young man with a light complexion and blonde hair. Although his mannerisms seem easygoing, he has a way of bringing out the best in one's performance. Under his direction, I fly the later part of my training until my proficiency warranted his recommendation for my flight test.

Even during homeroom school hour I study all

possible questions pertaining to the oral part of my test. I listen to my classmates brag about their favorite exploits, be it sports, or the most pronounced, automobiles. Most of them had at least a learner's permit; some had licenses, while only a few actually possessed an automobile. The majority know I do not posses any of these, thus leaving me the object of some ridicule.

On one occasion, I allow this to continue until I decide to interrupt them and inform them of my status. Unfortunately, there is no common ground for them to correlate their experiences to my flying experiences. Their unawareness of a dimension beyond the ground is evident in their questioning, and my attempts to answer fall on a few uninterested ears, while others listen in awe.

The sign on the door reads, Federal Aviation Administration. As I enter the hangar type building, I feel the official "government" atmosphere; metal framed windows, grey desks, black typewriters and generic tile floor. I am introduced to Mr. Grimes, chief inspector at the Albany, New York Office. I nervously sit down and present him with my paperwork, doing my best to make a good impression. He examines my application through very official looking glasses, supported by an equally official looking round face topped with thin graying hair. After carefully placing the papers on his desk, he starts asking questions regarding my airplane.

"How do you find the useful load of your airplane?"

This is my chance. I proceed to explain in great detail the proper weight and balance procedure; the center of gravity range down to the tenth of an inch; pilot; passenger and baggage weights, and moments as calculated aft of the aircraft datum; gasoline and oil located ahead of this measuring point results in with negative moments, using the simple formula...

He very politely interrupts me, "Ahhm, I am impressed with your understanding of the fine points. All I want to know is how you would arrive at the useful load of your airplane?"

My feeling of embarrassment is written all over my red face. I reply sheepishly, "Uh, oh those, subtract the empty weight from the gross weight."

"That is correct." After the oral is complete, I call for a weather briefing. Surface winds were gusting in excess of 25 knots. Although I do not want to cancel the flight, I know this to be the wisest decision, and for this he compliments me. "When you return, you will take your flight check with Mr. Brickman."

Upon my return the following week, I am seated and asked to wait for Mr. Brickman. Within a few moments I notice a very striking looking man with sandy hair, standing about 5' 10', shirt and tie and neatly pressed pants with a serious governmental expression on his face, approaching the desk.

"Sit down; let's take a look at your paper work." As he speaks, I detect a slight growl through his thick Maine accent. "Looks like you're one of Don's boys. How are things over at Loudon International?"

"Fine Sir."

"According to your application, we will be flying a high performance Cub." I look at him inquisitively, he knows it only has 65 horsepower. Not wanting to embarrass myself again, I say nothing.

With a slight hint of a smile, I pick up on his dry sense of humor. After a little more conversation, I realize this to be the façade of a man who "has been there and done that." I present to him my flight plan to Oneonta;

"Seems satisfactory." With that, he stands up, reaches for his hat and announces to his secretary his intentions of doing a little aviating.

The preflight went as planned, after taxiing to runway 19, we are cleared for take off on course to Oneonta.

Once established on course, I set the throttle for a normal cruise setting of 2250 RPM. I am asked to identify my location, and then deviate to an airfield just southwest of Albany. Approaching Mosher's field, things begin to get a little interesting. The engine is not running as smooth as before, and my check of the tachometer confirms my suspicion. The engine is only producing 1900 RPM.

At first I thought this to be part of the test; looking toward the back seat I check Brickman. He seems almost oblivious to the situation as he checks our position looking out the right side of the airplane. I check for carburetor ice, nothing. Fuel valve full on. Magneto check indicates a 100-RPM drop on each mag, as opposed to the normal 25-RPM drop. This concerns me. The roughness continues for a few more seconds, and then as suddenly as it started, the engine resumes normal operation. Since the problem seems to have disappeared, I cautiously continue the flight.

I check the winds at Mosher's field, the roughness presents itself again. This time to a much lesser degree, ending as fast as it began. I turn around to see an unconcerned Mr. Brickman. Again I continue with the flight. Moments later, for a third time, the roughness is back, a little more pronounced and accompanied by a slight tremor throughout the airplane. This is not part of the test. Nervously I proceed to check all I can from my vantage point. How can this go unnoticed to Brickman? With conviction in his voice he answers my question, "I got it! This f---ing thing is going to quit!"

Eloquent or not I am inclined to agree with him. Turning around I realize he is contemplating an unrehearsed forced landing.

After a few moments, which seem like an eternity, things settle down. Then to my complete surprise Brickman motions for me to continue the flight test. Without hesitation, I climb to a more suitable altitude, with a determination to fly better than I have ever flown before. After demonstrating slow flight, several stalls, and step turns, I am handed the hood.

Half way through the instrument portion of the test, we are once again held hostage to our renegade engine. Even the instrument panel has a slight shake as the engine losses power and returns to normal. I briefly hold my breath and literally cross my fingers as Brickman makes an announcement, "Alright, turn on your radio and fly us back to Albany. I will handle the throttle!"

Once established on the Albany Low Frequency Range, I turn slightly in my seat. This move allows me to see Brickman's reflection on the glass face of the oil pressure and temperature gauge. Placing his hat on his head and rendering the headset onto his knee, his expression reveals that this is not one of his better days.

Crossing the cone of silence, I expect to be directed to land at Albany. Instead, yet another surprise; I am directed to head for Loudon Airport, where I am to demonstrate several take off and landing procedures.

I put forth a little more effort during the simulated forced landings, half expecting any one of them to be the real thing. A small group gathers to watch all this, no doubt with a little apprehension. Should I pass, I will be the youngest Private Pilot in the area. I am sure there would be a lot more apprehension if everyone on the ground knows what the two of us in the airplane know.

We return to Albany for the final landing and completion of the flight test. Once on the ramp, Brickman crawls out of the Cub; in front of the FAA office, where he begins removing the lower engine cowling. This is a very interesting sight; an inspector, white shirt, tie, hat and the lower half of a Cub cowling in his hand with not one spot of grease on his clothes!

After inspecting the engine, I help him replace the engine cowling amid his grumbling over his lunch. We retire to the small coffee shack. The only conversation during lunch is a request for the telephone number at Loudon Airport.

After returning to the FAA office, Brickman

promptly calls Don. His description and mimicking the sound of our engine is almost comical, as he expresses the fact that we are both happy to be on the ground in spite of our desire to continue to fly.

"Your boy is fine, which is a hell of a lot more than I can say for your airplane," he says with a half smile, looking at me for a reaction, which is one big grin.

"When you come over here, come into my office, I'll explain more."

That said, he walks over to the secretary and asks her to fill out my temporary pilot certificate. I want to hoot, holler and jump up and down, but manage to control myself. A few moments later he sits down at his desk, looking me squarely in the eye.

"If you fly that Cub out of here, that will be the end of this piece of paper," he warns while holding up my certificate... "get to know the VOR as well as you do the low frequency range, because the day is coming when all four course radio ranges will be decommissioned."

The conversation between Don and Brickman is simple; the FAA wants to see better-equipped airplanes on flight tests, with more emphasis on full panel instrument training and better radios.

I am the last person to take a flight test at Albany in a Cub.

A later conversation with Don makes me realize Brickman is as much in favor of my passing as anyone. Don remarks; "I don't believe he actually let you continue the test after all that." Apparently I had made a better impression on Mr. Brickman than I thought, in spite of my nervousness.

For many years afterward, Mr. Brickman followed my career, both personally and professionally.

It was discovered that the cause for our problems were the piston rings on two of the cylinders which had started to seize. As a result, the engine was overhauled. After disassembly, I was informed that the engine probably would not have completely failed. I take comfort in this knowledge, however late it may be, and often wonder if the engine knew that.

Now I realize that it is time for a driver's license; I am getting tired of the mile and a half walk from the bus stop at Boght Corners to the airport.

E. A. Chevrette, Jr.

Chapter Four

In Search of a Friend

Small airports are fast becoming full time businesses and are slowly shedding their barnstorming image. People are beginning to realize that an airplane with less than four engines and carrying fewer than sixty people is not a Piper Cub. Business travel in light aircraft is now an everyday event, with places such as New York and Boston a mere hour away. Sponsored by an industry that is creating a large demand for its products and services, there is a well-organized campaign bringing this to the public's attention. We do not have the agenda, funding, or facilities of either the airlines or military; however, we encompass flight training, sight seeing, charter flights, crop dusting, and everything not offered by any other segment of aviation. As a result we are called General Aviation.

I experience first hand two worlds: the simple fun to fly airplane that is great for punching holes in the sky; and the faster, more sophisticated machines used for getting somewhere fast.

The newer breed of the airplane is replacing even the more plush, wood and fabric aircraft, such as the Fairchild, and Stagger-Wing Beechcrafts, flown mainly by the more affluent of the aviation community. With an emphasis on better reliability, stronger airframes, greater speeds and more comfort, even the new basic trainers have side-by-side seating, and cruise at 110 mph with a compliment of instruments and radios.

Loudon Airport now has two new airplanes. The first, a new modernized Piper Tri-Pacer. The other is a completely new airplane, the Piper Comanche; a high performance, 250 hp all metal sleek, low wing airplane. It is not only the first airplane on the field with retractable landing gear; it is the first airplane on the field to cruise at nearly 180 mph. The day this machine arrives on the field, it is love at first sight.

Equipped with a full instrument panel, and a compliment of crystal-controlled radios (14), this plane boasts comfortable seating with an interior color coordinating to the exterior paint scheme. Even servicing this airplane is different; I no longer need a ladder to fill each wing tank.

Shortly after receiving the new airplane, Don arranges for me to fly the Comanche with Kenney Derringer to North Adams and back. Keeping up with the higher speed, operating propeller and landing gear controls, along with the upscale electronic equipment, I feel as if I am flying a small airliner. The Comanche proves very popular among charter customers, business pilots and individuals, and is destined to become one of the most popular single engine airplanes of its day.

Whether it be a Comanche or Cub, new or old, anytime someone on the field purchases an airplane it is a call for some excitement and comradery. On this particular day, Tex, strolling into the hangar, announces his purchase of the silver Cub that sits at the end tie down, second row back.

After a discussion with Don concerning its

maintenance history, his purchase offer is accepted - $1200.00.

A group of us walk over to where the airplane is parked and begin to untie the ropes; here Tex asks Stan if he would give the airplane a test flight, to which Stan agrees. After a good preflight, both men climb aboard. With two pulls on the prop, the engine is running. As the airplane departs and proceeds to gain altitude over the airport, our small group heads for the hangar. I hear a voice originating from the hangar, "Hey Eddie, look!" In response, I look up to where everyone is pointing.

Once at altitude, Stan commences with an impromptu show. From level flight, the aircraft rolls over onto its back, then a split "S" recovery toward the ground. A loop, followed by a roll, continuing into a Cuban "8", (15) followed by a spin, then a dead stick landing for good measure. What an exhilarating demonstration of the mastery of flight.

After the flight, a discussion of some of these maneuvers proves quite interesting, especially among the experienced. Kenny Derringer discusses the day his father, also a flight instructor, initiated him into these maneuvers. He explains it started with a three-turn spin recovery, continuing into a loop, which was followed by a roll. With that said, Stan, Don and several other pilots engage in this conversation about the loop. They describe it as follows: on the first try, if there is not sufficient airspeed over the top, one will invariably end up with the dirt that is on the floor in your face. This tells you two things; one, you need more practice doing your loops;

two, your housekeeping is not up to par. I do not fully appreciate this until I try one.

Impromptu hangar flying sessions are even more interesting, particularly when they remind us of the barnstorming heritage. Tex, usually the object of much ridicule, peers over his thick glasses while rolling a cigarette made from pipe tobacco, and discusses the days when the only prerequisite for landing was the ability to stop short of the largest cow in the field. "Yep, you just looked which way the dust is blowing, or which way the grass was laying down and that gave us the wind direction."

Being the old time pilot he is, Tex frequently flies to Bennington, VT, usually inviting me along to fly his airplane and gain more flying time. He never takes any money for gas.

Ted, who has a strange resemblance to Icabod Crane, sits on the sofa next to Tex. While moving his hat around his head, he casually mentions his old Cub and the spins and loops he occasionally indulged in. Turning to Tex with his hat slightly askew, "I thought you told me your father didn't want you landing in that field anymore?" The two of them went back and forth with this while the rest of us laughed.

Ted has a subtle way of luring one into a joke, as I note one day while describing the uniqueness of the new instructor who is joining our airport. I sit in awe when he asks if I am interested in seeing the instructor's picture. As part of his joke, he then proceeds to open the centerfold of a Playboy Magazine. I do not know who has the redder face, him or me. Although his appearance and mannerisms make him seem unassuming, he possesses a Commercial Pilot License and is quite masterful at the controls of an airplane.

Dave Wallace, who is in the process of acquiring his instrument rating in his own Cessna 140, has just returned from a flight with Kenney Derringer. At this moment, he cannot resist getting into this conversation, "Just think Tex, when I get my instrument rating, you and I can fly on days when the birds are walking." His hearty laughter does not seem to fit his 5'5" physique as he brushes back his thinning hair and adjusts his rimless glasses. Turning toward me Dave asks, "How much flying have you done today? We have got to get you into the airlines. That is where you young fellows belong." He knows this is my ultimate dream. He has followed my flying since day one and along with his encouragement, I fly with him in his airplane regularly.

Keenan Duncan who is in his late twenties, quiet spoken, hair always neatly combed and parted on the side, enters the office. He has shared flying time with me in his Taylorcraft and is now joining Don and Kenney in conversation at the counter.

When in discussion, Don always uses his index figure to help make his point. Keenan looks out the window at the Comanche and states, "Now that is what I call an airplane. I bet you don't want to land that with the gear up."

Kenney looks at Keenan, "Makes it hard to taxi off the runway if you do."

These conversations continue on until we are all

laughed out.

While all of this is going on, I stand back a moment to reflect.

Should a stranger overhear this conversation, they would not understand why any of us were allowed anywhere near an airplane, let alone fly one. In reality, this is their façade; a way of sharing a special moment. For below the surface, their friendship and flying are taken very seriously.

It was a warm August afternoon when I arrive at the airport. Entering the hangar, I can sense something is very wrong. Don is pacing back and forth just inside the open hangar doors, alternately puffing and chewing on his cigarette. Stan and Tex are huddled near the office door; neither man is smiling. A few of the local pilots and aircraft owners are gather around the Tri-Pacer engaged in a discussion inaudible from my location.

Walking into the office, Don calls my attention, and with a painful expression, he explains the circumstances. The day before, Dave Wallace and Don had discussed the eastbound weather as Dave was contemplating a trip to Beverly, Mass. to visit friends and family. That morning, a weak front had passed through the Berkshires and Don's concern was the uplifting effect the mountains have on the westerly winds. This can cause, at the least, rapid mountaintop obscurations, or at best summertime thunderstorms.

After their discussion, Dave decided to take a short flight for a look at the eastbound weather and probably postpone his trip until the next day. He was expected to return in an hour. Something must have changed. That conversation was yesterday.

Today, Dave has still not returned to Loudon, nor did he ever arrive at Beverly.

When I hear the news, I look toward the tie down where Dave keeps his blue and white Cessna 140. Three ropes lay neatly wound around each tie down ring, evidence of his neatness and expectations of returning home. I am stunned. I cannot believe this is happening; Dave is not prone to carelessness. Not having planned more than a local flight, he did not exercise his option and file a flight plan. Normally, at the end of the flight, if the flight plan is not closed, a phone search is conducted one hour after the ETA. If this does not produce any results, Search and Rescue is then notified along with Police authorities, Civil Air Patrol and all airports along the flight. Dave had not intended more than a local flight, and without a flight plan, search and rescue operations are delayed.

Once it is determined that we have a missing airplane on our hands, the search becomes official, and is in high gear. Our visitors include the State Police, FAA officials, Civil Air Patrol, pilots from neighboring airports and the press. We are getting notoriety, the likes of which is not welcome. There seems to be an invisible accusing finger demanding atonement for all who fly.

Even though there is no concrete proof of Dave's whereabouts, everyone who thinks they know something about aviation is suddenly an expert with all the answers, none of which are pertinent. This small airstrip north of Cohoes is getting high profile coverage. We grow tired of the rhetoric in a big hurry; this pilot is one of our own and we want answers, not more ignorant suppositions.

By the time the official search is underway, we have already initiated our own. We are all infuriated as one official informs us that we are not trained to search for aircraft, and should not interfere. To this we express our position quite poignantly: this is personal; we are not looking for an airplane, we are in search of a friend.

Everyone at the airport joins in on the search. Individual owner pilots flew their own airplanes with their family members as observers. Don uses the Cessna 170, personally asking people to occupy a seat. Our own families volunteered as observers. I fly the Tri-Pacer, sometimes with Stan, sometimes with local pilots or neighbors. If Tex, Ted, Kenny, Tom, and Richard, can get their hands on a vacant airplane they'll fly it.

Tex fly's his Cub within a 25-mile range of Loudon, while aircraft with greater range capability fly searches farther from the airport. Richard, who has access to a Navion, on one occasion flies a four-hour search. Don flies in similar fashion in the Cessna 170; I am in between with the Tri-Pacer. Others fly what they can.

Between flights, while refueling, we huddle together in the office to exchange information. Our clothing soaked with perspiration leads some of us to the lavatory to splash cool water on our faces. Others hastily eat a half sandwich and share a cold coke. At one point, one of the officials mentions to Don that he had underestimated our group. Without acknowledgement, Don finishes his sandwich and prepares for another flight.

We cover small towns in the foothills of the Berkshires, sometimes between mountains where the peaks are higher than the airplane. We considered turbulence a mere nuisance, the occasional stray thunderstorm we circumnavigate. When an observer sights a reflection or something unusual on the ground, the pilot immediately flies over the site, sometimes requiring steep banks or "non-standard" maneuvers trying to get into position for a better look. This is often followed by a maneuver in the opposite direction, each time hoping we find our man. This only results in tired pilots and sick observers.

Our efforts continue for several days without results. In the evening, everyone helps secure the aircraft either in the hangar or at their respective tie downs. As we gather in groups, fatigue and frustration is all we have to show for our efforts.

One evening, I, as well as others, notice Don standing in front of the hangar slowly puffing on a cigarette, while looking toward Bald Mountain and the east. We all know what he is thinking. Our silence a unanimous vote in agreement: this is no longer a search and rescue operation. The best we can hope for is retrieval, but where and when?

The officials keep searching for a little more than a week, at which point they too realize that any chances of survival are bleak. There is a somber mood in our hangar sessions and ideas as to where he might be are diminishing.

Although we still have a small tinge of hope, reality makes us realize there is nothing more we can do. It is time to get on with our lives and the business of flying.

The rest of the summer passed without incident.

One early fall day, we received the official word, and the answer to our question: Dave had been found and there were no survivors. But the shocking news is where he was found. The accident site is on a farm near Colrain Massachusetts; this placed him on the eastern fringe of the Berkshires. He had almost reached his destination; no one involved in the search had even come close to where he was found. Somehow, he had gotten passed most of the weather and in a few more minutes would have probably been in the clear. We all ask the same question, " why?"

The following week, Dave's silent partner in the airplane, Gary Monelli, and a few others decide to drive to the site to see if anything is salvageable. I am invited to go along.

The drive to Colrain is quite lengthy, especially since one of the vehicles was an old Dodge flatbed. When we arrive at the farm, the owner, a very elderly man of frail health, greets us. After all the introductions, he explains how his family, while hiking on their property, found the wreckage. After his offer to take us on the mile and a half hike to the site, his daughter informs us that he has a heart condition. On top of everything else, we do not need a heart attack victim on our hands. After a brief discussion, the daughter and her husband, who had found the wreckage agreed to take us to the site. As we hike into the woods, I have no idea what to expect and do my best to keep apprehension in check.

When we arrive, we all stand in a silence. After a few moments, one by one we speak as we begin to survey the site. This is a heavily wooded area; a site that would be next to impossible to locate from the air. Looking up the only sign I can see of anything coming through the trees is one small broken limb, which could have been caused by nature.

From the limb, I follow an imaginary line to the first point of impact, at the base of a large oak tree. The impact was so hard the left wing is sheared at the wing root and is completely wrapped around the tree. The wing tip and the end of the external wing strut are almost touching each other on the opposite side of the tree. This is unbelievable. If the property owner's sense of direction for North is accurate, Dave was heading in an easterly direction when he hit the top of the trees. After the initial impact, the aircraft continued for another hundred feet or so until the right wing was sheared by another tree, after which the aircraft came to rest, nose down, upon two trees so close together that what was left of the aircraft could not pass. The top of the fuselage then split open and at this point the seat belt sheared on the pilot's side and Dave was thrown another fifty feet beyond the wreckage. Walking toward what I thought to be where Dave landed, I inquire of the son of the property owner about a strange odor.

"Don't go any further, you will be standing where we found the pilot, or what was left of him."

I turned around to a sight that to this day I will never forget. There are actual skeletal remains of his fingers on the ground in front of me. For the most part, what is left of him had been placed in a bag for retrieval and examination the previous week. At this point, I feel a cold chill run up my spine and am shocked at my curiosity that wants to know more about what put him here. What led up to this tragic loss of a good friend? Could it have been avoided? How?

Suddenly, in the background I heard Gary's loud voice expressing anger and utter frustration. As I approach him and the property owner to get a grasp of the situation, I am shocked at what I hear. Gary is standing in front of the older man and almost screaming for an explanation.

"Why has this instrument panel been stripped?

Gary holds the metal instrument panel in his hand, although in relatively good condition it was barren of all flight instruments. Another pilot in our group tries to explain that with such an impact there would be no way anyone could tell if someone had removed the instruments. Even if that were the case, what good would they be to anyone?

I knew the airplane was considered one of the best-equipped Cessna 140's around. Could someone have actually found this site, stripped the instrument panel and not have told anyone? We also knew Dave had a considerable amount of cash with him; of which little was found. I find this whole scenario quite disturbing.

The decision is made to remove the engine. Possibly this can be salvaged. The engine is tied to a makeshift rig-

ging between two poles, and as a group we return to the vehicles. The return drive led to other questions. Why would
this man venture this far if the weather was not favorable?
We know he was working toward his instrument rating.
Even though he had not officially taken any flight test, he
had enough training and experience to at least fly the airplane should he encounter less favorable weather conditions. An autopsy at this stage is out of the question, so we
will never know if he suffered an attack of some kind. The
questions continue almost endlessly, all without answer.

The only evidence of a probable cause is that this
definitely had all the earmarkings of a graveyard spiral,
which again points to the fact that he should have been
able to handle the situation at least to the point of
recovery.

Upon our arrival at Loudon, Don takes one look
at the engine and shakes his head.... "Should have left it
there!"

After everyone leaves, I discussed with Don what I
had witnessed.

"What do you make of it?" I ask. He lights a cigarette,
and in the light of the match, I can see the seriousness
and the sorrow in his face and I realize he is not a stranger
to such a loss. He speaks quietly, at first looking at the
floor, then directly at me, "Well, sometimes these things
happen. A mistake in judgment, an oversight, bad luck,
call it what you may. These machines are not toys, and
anything that has the capability of killing you deserves a
lot of respect. It is a hard thing to say what a man is going
to do when the chips are down, and a damn poor time to

find out that we play for keeps. Time has a way of testing us all, some for the good, and otherwise. In a way, it is good that you are learning this early. Whether you accept this or not is up to you."

We discuss the missing instruments. It is pointed out that as bad as the impact was, there still should have been remnants of the damaged instrument casings. When asked if we found any, I just shake my head no.

As I walk across the gravel parking lot, I cannot help but think that something like this always happens to the other guy; not so. This one hit home. Investigators, pilots and mechanics can explain in very technical terms how things happen and how to avoid them; usually accomplished in a Monday morning quarterback session. However, all the great minds in aviation can never fully explain the sorrow felt by the loss of a friend.

Chapter Five

Seasons of Change

Fall arrives and the changing leaves make a kaleidoscope of the countryside with colors so vivid that at times it is difficult to keep my attention on flying the airplane. I find this to be particularly true during cross-country flights I fly in pursuit of my Commercial Pilots License. Although qualified in faster airplanes, the Cub is still an economically appealing time builder.

On the days with almost limitless visibility, pilots are sometimes prone to being less critical of their navigation and occasionally select irrelevant checkpoints too far from the airplane. This can result in over flying one's destination. However, when in-flight visibility is reduced by haze, smoke or precipitation, a pilot must fly lower and use checkpoints closer to the airplane. This is done to minimize the chance of missing a checkpoint and getting disorientated. I soon find myself adapting rapidly to these situations.

Flying the Hudson Valley on a hazy day, from a distance the Catskills seem to take on a different shape. The refraction caused by the thick haze tends to hide their true shape, as they appear more rectangular and layered as opposed to their normal protrusion against the horizon. This is a very different scene as compared to the Berkshires, which seem to lurk in the haze and suddenly jump out to pilots who venture close to them at low altitudes.

E. A. Chevrette, Jr.

Some days this haze layer is thick and extends high enough that ground contact can be maintained only by looking straight down which also makes visual contact with other aircraft difficult. On the occasion when I have the capability of climbing on top of this intrusion to visibility, I experience some slight turbulence (16) passing through its well-defined top layer. From this position I find smooth air and almost limitless visibility. While the haze may almost completely obscure the ground; the higher mountain peaks in the distance are a reminder there is still turf below.

Precipitation presents a different situation, although it too will cause me to fly closer to the ground. There is a slight added challenge when flying the Cub in a light rain shower. While looking through the side window on the door, I watch the caked mud on the landing gear leg turn into a liquid then travel with the moving air until it disappears. Rain flowing around the windshield will invariably leak through the leading edge of the door and run across the inside of the window, with a few drops reaching the floor and my right sleeve. The plop-plop on the chart held in my lap is from the leak over my head where the top of the windshield joins the fuselage. I protect my chart by placing it behind my back against the seat, holding it up briefly for a navigation check. As a pilot I will endure such a test while flying this airplane; however, I will be the first to complain about the leaky roof while standing in the hangar.

A west or northwest wind over the Catskills usually produces, at the least, an uncomfortable ride. This subsequent turbulence continues at altitudes high enough to affect the commercial flights from Albany southbound. Turbulence is an unpredictable phenomenon you never know when you might run into it. Air flows over the terrain much the same way as water flows down stream with some of the heaviest turbulence produced after passing the rough terrain. The trick is to visualize this when flying over mountains, thus steering well clear of the downwind side of the higher peaks. I learn this rather quickly, particularly on occasion where I spend as much time retrieving the chart as I do reading it.

The Berkshires play host to several airfields, one in particular is North Adams, Massachusetts, and its east west runway that lies at the northern base of Mt. Greylock. North Adams is home to a commercial operation, a corporate flight department, and is also an excellent location for the local glider club. On this particular afternoon, I find myself standing next to the Cub watching the gliders make their silent flight up the mountainside. Once free of the updrafts they soar peacefully in the clear sky over the airport. I find this appealing.

During a discussion with one of the local glider pilots, he explains some of the techniques used to find these thermals. His reward is clearing the 3,491-foot summit of Mt. Greylock, which is topped with a 92-foot granite Memorial Tower commemorating the casualties of all the wars (17).

Upon my departure I decide to give one of the soaring techniques a try. Although the Cub is considerably heavier, it is not much more than a glider with an engine and I think the try is worth the effort. After departing the traffic pattern, I head for the windward side of the mountain. On my first attempt, I fly through a few pockets of light turbulence without any signs of altitude gain. I continue circling until I experience more noticeable turbulence; it is here, according to my altimeter, the airplane is starting to gain altitude.

As I continue circling I find I can actually reduce the power to 1,900 RPM, lower the nose slightly, and continue gaining altitude. Within a few minutes my altimeter reads 3,700 feet as I look down on the winding road leading to the granite tower. I can just imagine the feeling of accomplishment reaching this same altitude without an engine.

Not all days find cloudless skies over Mt. Greylock. When clouds obscure the mountains around North Adams, the only way in or out is to visually follow the valley that runs from Bennington, Vermont, and continues past the eastern end of the runway at North Adams. While accomplishing this task, two things are important; good visibility, and being the only airplane navigating the valley.

Even the birds are part of the changing seasons. On a few occasions I happen upon a flock of migrating fowl. Two such incidents prove quite interesting. While flying northeast of Saratoga Lake, I suddenly engage in a steep turn to avoid collision with a flock of geese while simultaneously, the geese are performing their own evasive maneuvering. I am impressed when I discover the flock has resumed their formation prior to my recovering from my steep turn. To satisfy my curiosity, I decide to follow the flock and observe. Not able to fly the airplane that slow, twice I try to gain a closer look by circling the flock. I can only marvel at their ability to regroup and resume their original track, which is faster than I can turn the airplane around. There have been collisions with birds of this size causing considerable damage to an airplane, and in some cases worse. As fun as this is, I proceed with caution.

A few days later, I happen upon a flock of duck in the same vicinity. On this particular day, the base of the clouds is measured at three thousand feet. As the birds navigate southward, a few venture into the cloud cover. I watch rather intently for the results; within a matter of seconds each duck tumbles uncontrollably out of the clouds earthbound. I laugh as this scenario is repeated twice more with the same results. Here is positive proof that all things that fly have limitations, even the birds.

The onset of shorter days sparks our interest in night flying. Although Loudon is strictly a daytime operation, desire and ingenuity provide for limited nighttime operation. Any night flying originating and returning to Loudon requires us to set up our own lighting system, which consists of approximately a dozen nine-volt battery operated lanterns. Utilizing white, green and red colored lenses, these low intensity lights are hand placed at strategic locations around the runway perimeter. Although not exactly Government Issue, they work. On occasion, when only one airplane is landing after dark, as is the case when Kenney returns from a charter, we use a slightly different technique. We strategically park a car at the threshold of the active runway, the taillights marking the end of the runway while the headlights illuminate the touchdown zone.

The landing lights of the aircraft on final approach shine in through the rear window. Waiting and listening for the engine to pass, what seems like inches overhead the car, the aircraft then appears in front of the automobile. The actual touchdown is made in the area illuminated by the headlights and then the aircraft would roll into the darkness with only the aircraft landing lights for guidance. I think it takes as much courage to sit in the automobile as it does to land the airplane.

Before departing Loudon on my first night flight with Stan, I adjust the two small overhead lights toward the instrument panel and away from the windshield. In the darkened cockpit, each instrument on the panel reflects the subdued red light. I synchronize the numbers on the Directional Gyro to match those on the compass, and set the altimeter to field elevation. The checklist is complete; the stage is now set and the command performance is about to begin.

It is a clear night as we depart northward toward Saratoga Springs, New York. The steady drone of the engine as it pulls the wing through smooth solid air, while the lights of a small village slide underneath, is almost hypnotic. The next area of darkness is ended by a display of lights defining straight avenues and streets, starting in darkness and ending the same; all precisely outline the geographic boundaries of the city. Turning southbound from Saratoga Springs, I head toward Albany Airport.

Looking out the windshield on a night that supports a full moon and a sky full of bright stars is living proof of one of the priceless rewards one finds when leaving the ground.

Navigating toward Albany, I soon see the alternating green and white flashing colors of the airport beacon; I contact the tower for all information pertinent to our arrival. I will now be introduced to a whole new world of lights; the tower has activated the high intensity approach lights for runway 19. The sequentially flashing strobe lights are unmistakingly airport-oriented and easy to find (18).

I am now on final approach to a runway cloaked in total darkness whose only clue of existence are the lights around its perimeter. I will not see its surface until I cross the green threshold lights. As my landing light illuminates the runway surface, I get the illusion of traveling at a much higher speed. I can almost feel myself holding my breath in anticipation of the wheels touching the runway, for this is another first, and the start of a new column in my logbook.

Our next destination is Schenectady, not as well equipped, but with less traffic which affords more time for night take off's and landing practice. This includes learning to land at night without the aid of aircraft landing lights.

Departing Loudon presented little difficulty, our eyes were accustomed to the low intensity lighting; however, returning from Schenectady or Albany is a different story. Departing Latham, I reference the streetlights and use radio navigation as a back up. In order to follow State Route 9 north of Boght Corners I use the reflections of headlights on the highway. Dimming the instrument lights to minimize reflections on the windows, I start to look for the dark void where I see the night light overhead the hangar door, and from there, looking slightly to the east are the runway lights.

Using the Albany altimeter setting I align the airplane with Route 9 and then fly the pattern until the airplane is on final approach between the rows of lanterns outlining the runway. Double-checking the altimeter and airspeed, I wait to get a glimpse of the power lines south of the runway. Here I continue my approach to cross the runway threshold between two red lanterns. When the landing lights reflect off the gravel runway, I reduce the power and hold back on the wheel and wait for the main gear to touch home turf.

After this session we enter the office, where the bright overhead light seems a rude conclusion to our night flight. We discuss the changing seasons and predictable weather changes, noting that the end of this season marks a big physical change to our airport. A large assembly plant and warehouse for agricultural tractors and equipment has become our new neighbor. This change is not as predictable.

The Plant and warehouse building are located on the southwest corner of the airport where the two runways intersect, consuming part of the south end of the runway and the entire tie-down area south of the main taxiway. The outside storage area is fenced in adjacent to our main taxiway, making for careful travel in and out of the hangar and gas pumps.

Another runway is built on the west side of the existing one starting on the northeast corner of the plant and intersecting the existing runway midfield. After some tree removal, an extension is added to the north end of the airport, giving us a slight dogleg between the existing runway and its northern extension. The changes allow us limited use of the original runway, and the northern extension for those operations requiring operations to the south runway. For the moment, our interests lie with the seasonal changes, while thoughts of what the upcoming seasons would mean to the future of the airport unanswered.

Winter brings with it the usual "nor'easters" with bitter temperatures and soul piercing winds. This particular one is followed by two days of strong surface winds, some with gusts exceeding 55 miles per hour. These gusts are so strong I can hear the entire metal roof on the hangar ripple in response. Manipulating the hangar doors in such conditions requires at least three people; one to close the door, and two others to hold onto the operator. This same wind drifts the snow against the fence and all but hides the taxiway.

Two days later, Don and I return from a trip to North Adams in the Tri-Pacer. From an altitude of three thousand feet I can see remnants of the blowing and drifting of snow over the mountains. While adjusting the front heater, Don takes notice of the outside air temperature gauge - minus forty degrees. At this temperature both Celsius and Fahrenheit are numerically equal. It is extremely cold for this altitude, giving me a greater appreciation for Piper, Lycoming and whoever made the cabin heater.

Completing the landing roll on the west runway, we taxi to the hangar on what is left of the original north runway. As we pass the huge block wall of the warehouse, there are no words exchanged.

The smell of freshly brewed coffee as we enter the office is a great way to make one feel at home. As I start removing my winter garb, layer by layer, Ted begins the conversation. We discuss the possibility of the airport becoming a part of a new industrial complex, with paved runways, new hangars and permanent lighting; a sort of rebirth of an airport, opposite of the expected demise. Our excitement and hopes only disguise our fears. The addition of the plant to our airport has already taken up more room than expected, causing each of us more concern than we care to admit. This year the seasons of change will also bring a new challenge.

Spring has arrived, and with it the mud season. The sod covered west runway is normally unusable this time of year. However, this year the mud has rendered the new extension of the runway to the north unusable, as well as the southern portion of the original runway, located behind the plant. Only the short section of the new runway between the plant and where it intersects the original runway is usable which is approximately 800 feet. The width of the runway in some locations is about that of the wingspan of most of the airplanes, or approximately 36 feet.

The other half of the equation involves the March winds that under normal conditions require good crosswind technique. With the building and the runway in such close proximity, we are not yet sure how much turbulence to expect from these west winds flying so close to the building.

It is obvious we must devise a tactic that will allow us the best use of our limited resources; we will have to maneuver the airplanes in such a manner to permit touching down as close to the end of the new runway as possible. Being a resourceful bunch, we decide to fly around the building instead of over it.

Flying the approach to the north means aligning with the existing runway behind the building. Once arriving at what used to be our touchdown area, power is applied to keep the airplane airborne just below building height. Once we reach the northeast corner of the building, we side step around the building against the wind and onto the new section of runway. Then we maneuver over the new section of runway, reducing the sideslip and power, while retracing the flaps contacting the ground left gear first. Once on the ground, the next step is stopping the machine before running out of useable runway. Upon completion of this "non-standard technique", we manually push the machine backwards toward the taxiway or into position for another takeoff.

Learning this technique in the Cessna 172 proves an interesting experience, as is evident on one windy Sunday afternoon. On my first attempt at approaching the corner of the building, I experience some slight turbulence as I proceed to add power and cross control the airplane in order to start the side step maneuver. Once over the runway, I reduce the power and allow only the main gear to touch before adding power and commencing a go around. This first try is mainly a confidence builder - the second try Don directs me to plan for a full stop landing.

On the final approach for a second try, I notice the windsock indicating an increase in wind velocity directly out of the west. Approaching the corner of the building I add power as before, but this time with a little twist. I hit a wind gust of such intensity relative to the ground that the airplane is almost stationary. My head hits the side window, while at the same time both Don and I have pushed the throttle fully open to attempt a go around. With full power, I am literally wrestling with the airplane to keep it airborne at just above a stall and avoid settling into the mud, which could prove hazardous under these conditions. After a few tense moments, I have completed a successful go around and return for another approach and a new found respect for March winds.

After retiring the airplanes for the day, Ted, while pouring a cup of coffee, looks at me with a half smile on his face, "Ahhaa rather sporting out there today isn't it?" Although somewhat enjoying the new challenge both winter and spring bring, we welcome summer with open arms.

What is considered entertaining to us may not be looked upon in the same light by others; at least not initially. Such is the case on this beautiful summer Sunday afternoon. The skies are clear and a slight south wind embraces the airport. In the parking lot, aviation enthusiasts of all ages are watching the airplanes and enjoying the afternoon. This includes one familiar older couple that only ventures out to the airport after consuming a certain amount of "liquid courage."

In a half-serious discussion we wonder how many of them we could interest in taking flying lessons. After a few laughs, we agree that the most interesting part of flying with us is getting used to our sense of humor.

"I wonder what we could do to really raise their interest." Don soon answers my question.

"Whatever you do, be careful. You might sober a couple of them up." This response produces another outburst of laughter. While watching the group hanging on the fence that divides the parking lot from the ramp, it is mentioned by a few (pointing to me), that I should get a "move on" for that Commercial License.

With that, Stan and I discuss some of the required maneuvers, some of which are the simulated dead stick, spot landings, and the possibility of actually performing this maneuver a little more realistically. Looking at the people in the parking lot, with a half - smile on our faces, Stan and I prepare one of the Cubs 92210 for flight. He briefs me on the maneuver and its procedures.

Climbing to 2000 feet over the airport, we align ourselves with the south runway. Stan applies carburetor heat, closes the throttle, then reaches up and places the mag switch to the off position. I pull the nose up to slow the airspeed near stall and stop the wooden propeller from wind milling. Once accomplished, I lower the nose and maintain 65 mph. Stan, with a big grin on is face, opens the door and yells down for everybody to hear.

"Hey Mulligan, the engine quit." Sort of half-running, Don comes out toward the runway to look up. It does not take long for him to get the idea; I look down and can almost see him smiling. I know he has been here before.

All is silent except for the wind passing the airframe. The lack of power from the engine is also confirmed by a zero reading on the tachometer and a motionless wooden propeller staring back at me through the windshield.

"Always keep the field in sight, making your initial turns over the runway." We accomplish two 360-degree turns, followed by a 135-degree turn placing the runway just over and behind my left shoulder. I start the base leg and keep the approach on the high side. Once on final approach I slip the airplane toward the end of the runway and touch down just beyond our predetermined spot. Stan jumps out, props the engine and we are off again for another try.

"If you miss the spot this time, you buy the cokes."

In the meantime, Don and a few other pilots are discussing what we are doing in front of our potential customers, who by this time are asking questions faster than they could be answered. Most of the on lookers, including the older couple, took scenic flights, while two other onlookers actually sign up for lessons. Our marketing tactics must be working.

After tying down the airplane, I ask Stan how we would be charged for renting the airplane and logging flight time.

"Flight time is logged from the time the engine starts until you shut it down at the end of the flight."

"Do you think Don will give me a discount for this flight?" Stan laughs for a good minute on that one.

Shortly after this flight, Stan takes a leave of absence due to previous commitments. I use the remainder of the summer to finish my cross-country requirements, complete the written exam, and finish high school. The fall finds me attending evening business college and working during the day to provide the funds needed to complete my license.

It is a cold, early winter evening and we are operating out of Albany Airport to take advantage of some night flying. Dressed in winter garb, hats pulled over our eyes, collars rolled up to our ears, we sit in Don's car with only the dome light for illumination. The atmosphere in the car is almost that of three bootleggers planning their next heist. It is here, where I am formally introduced to my new mentor.

Sandy complexion, thinning hair with matching eyelashes, 5'9" tall, is Fred Carlsberg, also known as Sandy. As he looks at me out of the corner of his eye, I can almost hear the wheels turning. He listens to everything that is spoken; sometimes only showing acknowledgement with a quick nodding of his head, or blinking of his eyes from behind the smoke rising from his pipe. He looks away, then back again, almost as though I were under a microscope. He has the outward appearance of a quiet, laidback man. However, being a retired Navy Flight Instructor, I am soon to find his true spirit.

The airplane we use is a Cessna 150. Soon after takeoff, on our first flight together, there is a review of the basic maneuvers. After about thirty minutes, Fred takes over the controls.

"To start with, I consider plus or minus 50 feet on slow flight to be sloppy flying, steep turns included. Altitude loss in stall recovery needs to be cut in half."

He then proceeds to demonstrate. Flying the airplane just above the stall, the altimeter needle does not move, nor does the heading. Steep turns are to be executed with a sixty-degree bank instead of the usual forty-five, with little tolerance for change. Rolling from a steep bank to the left to one in the opposite direction will be completed on the same heading, with little or no altitude change. Stall recoveries are to be deliberate and smooth.

"There is one thing I do not want to see in this airplane - lazy feet." With a thirty-degree pitch attitude, he removes his feet from the rudder pedals. Pulling the control wheel to the full nose up position while correcting heading change with full right aileron, he makes his point perfectly clear; when the aircraft stalls, it rolls abruptly to the left, followed by the nose which is headed for the ground. Upon returning to level flight, with a slight grin on his face, he turns to me; "Your turn."

For the next several hours my work is cut out for me. Fred closely observes every move I make. As my performance approaches his limitations, he tightens the margin of error. On the ground, in between flights, he proceeds with elaborate details on each maneuver, while being very demonstrative in his verbal and physical descriptions. He often laughs and cajoles during these sessions only exemplifying the love he has for his work. He can also be quite firm, particularly if he detects any sloppiness in my work; this he will not tolerate.

These sessions are also the preview of what is to come.

I watch in awe as he demonstrates Chandelles and Lazy eights which require a higher degree of planning and coordination. My first attempt at these maneuvers brings a smile to his face or a quick laugh. Although he demands accuracy and precision, he also knows how to teach it. I am also learning that the addition of a little artistry into one's work is always welcomed.

Flying pylons near the ground demands tighter tolerances and greater concentration. Fred will occasionally chew on an apple while observing my work. As long as he chews his apple slowly, I know my work is acceptable; however, if his chewing rate increases, I know once he swallows what he has in his mouth, I am next.

One afternoon, he draws a circle in the gravel on the runway with a stick; this will be used for our spot landing work. Fred explains as he demonstrates the first one, "This circle has a twenty foot radius, once you get the idea, the next one will have a ten foot radius." With that, the two main wheels ever so gently touch the center of the circle. "As an added incentive, the winner will receive a ripe red apple." Because of this for the next few sessions I made it a point to bring apples to my flight lesson.

Instrument work with Fred proves no less demanding - heading changes beyond five degrees and altitudes that vary more than fifty feet on turbulent days is considered sloppy flying. Although we have attitude and directional gyro instruments, rarely is an entire flight made using all of them. If Fred does not physically cover one or more of them up, he will maneuver the aircraft in such a way to cause these instruments to tumble, rendering them useless. (19)

On several occasions, while under the hood, I am instructed to look down at my lap. Waiting for the command to look up and recover, I am pushed sideways in the seat, or feel the seat drop underneath me, or even momentarily hang on my belt. I must learn the discipline required to suddenly look up at an instrument panel, quickly and accurately determine what is being shown, and recover the aircraft back to level flight, all while at the same time ignoring my natural senses.

Lessons are split between the advanced maneuvers and instrument flying until Fred's work is apparent in my performance. One afternoon after a lengthy session, Fred checks all my paperwork then comments; "OK, great, fill out one of the recommendation forms for me to sign and call for an appointment. It is time for your check ride!" I am happy, surprised and a little nervous as I am directed to contact Mr. Guy Scram, an examiner in Glens Falls, New York.

The main terminal at Warren County Airport houses the waiting area and ticket counter for Mohawk Airlines. The main floor also shares a small coffee shop and rest rooms, where I stop to adjust my tie and comb my hair prior to my flight test.

On the second floor, there is a pilot briefing area, which includes the flight service and a great view of the ramp below. To the right of that doorway is a ladder that leads to the control tower atop the building, long since decommissioned. Across from the Flight Service Station is another door, which leads to the offices of Cape Aircraft. Once inside, I introduce myself to a tall thin man, 6' 3", mostly arms and legs. He wears a huge smile that lights up his whole face and emphasises the wrinkles and lines of experience that seem so well suited to him. He is so graceful and energetic, at one point I almost expect him to break out into song.

"How are things at Loudon? I have got to get out of here more often and stop by and see Don and all the boys." The conversation very nicely gets around to business. I present him my written test results, medical certificate and logbooks pertaining to the aircraft and engine, and of course my written recommendation. I am then asked to plot a course for Bradley International Airport, Windsor Locks, Connecticut, and prepare the necessary flight plan for the cross-country portion of the flight test.

We then enter the flight portion of the test. After takeoff I head for a planned destination. Once it is established that I can navigate, we proceed with the visual maneuvers; and then onto the instrument portion of the test. This culminates in a simulated forced landing with the ground reference maneuvers to follow. Upon our return, the test is commenced with a spot landing and we then retire to his office. After a few moments, he returns to his desk, "I guess I am going to send you home without your Private License." He laughs as he congratulates me and hands me my temporary Commercial Pilot License. I do not realize that this is also the start of a long-term relationship with Guy, both personal and professional, for this is not the last we will see of each other.

Upon my return home, climbing out of the airplane, I give a good 'ole thumbs up to everyone standing in the hangar. Fred and a few of the local constabulary come over to congratulate me. As the group walks into the hangar, I hear a voice from the back call out. " I see you do not have a Private License anymore." I turn; it is Don. I can only smile as I loosen my tie.

Suddenly I stop and look around. I must have a worried look on my face because Don remarks, "Relax, you've outgrown that bucket of water! Besides, that's a nice tie, wouldn't want to get it wet." This is followed by his usual laugh and a few congratulatory moments.

A few days later, I am given my first revenue producing assignment as a new Commercial Pilot; a scenic flight. Two children are belted into the back seat of the 172. Their uncle, a very large man, is having trouble occupying the right front seat of the airplane and actually gets stuck half way through the door. His right foot is on the step mounted on the right main landing gear, his left foot partially inside the airplane. The left side of his head is pushed up against the bottom of the right wing, with his right leg up against his right arm.

What is concerning, is that the doorway on the 172 is quite large, and under normal circumstances makes access into or out of the airplane relatively easy. It takes three of us to get him into the airplane amidst his complaining about his bad back. I am in the left seat pulling on his belt, while the mechanic and another pilot are standing outside the airplane pushing him toward me.

Once inside, the seat belts are just long enough to fasten him in. Due to the weight and temperature of the day, the airplane was not exactly overly enthusiastic about leaving the ground.

Shortly after takeoff, the two children in the back seat decide to unfasten their belts and take a tour of the airplane, while at the same time their uncle expresses his wishes to return to earth. Once clear of the airport, I mention to the uncle that he will have to fasten the children back into their seats. Looking at me out of the corner of his eye, while expressing his willingness to comply, he explains he cannot move even if he wanted to.

It is at this point that I turn around to survey the situation. The smallest girl has started to climb the back of the rear seat in an effort to reach the rear baggage compartment. The other one, on her hands and knees, has wedged herself between the two front seats in an effort to reach the fuel selector valve. Of all the manuals I have studied, nothing was ever mentioned about a situation like this one. After considerable manipulation I am able to refasten both small occupants into their respective seats.

Considering their size, it is difficult for either of them to look out the side windows without sitting on some elevation so I decide to bank a little more steeply to allow them to see. This keeps them occupied, but raises havoc with their uncle. I return to the airport after what has seemed a very long ten minutes. With the aid of two other people, our intrepid passengers are unloaded and returned to their earthbound habitants. Everyone has a good belly laugh over the whole scene, which is the talk of the airport for some time to come. I am even paid for my professionalism, two quarters, yes fifty cents is the entire amount the pilot is paid for a ten-minute scenic ride. I should have taken the hint.

Chapter Six

The Test of Time

Albany County Airport is now home to a new Crash Fire and Rescue building. The FAA General Aviation District Office, Flight Service Station, Weather Bureau and other offices associated with the airport, are now under one roof. As I climb the stairs to the second floor, I go over the paper work I have in my hand; among the documents is a written recommendation for a Certified Flight Instructors Flight Test signed by my flight instructor, Fred Carlsberg.

The required maneuvers for this rating are similar to those for the Commercial Pilot's License, with a few exceptions. First: there is the transition to flying from the right seat of the airplane, second; analyzing each maneuver, identifying common errors and applying the proper corrections; third: I never thought it possible, but Sandy actually demands an even higher level of proficiency in my flying.

As I approach his desk, he is sitting with his back to the room looking out the window. Turning toward me, a familiar Maine accent greets me, "Good Morning, I trust you brought with you an airplane that will run smoothly for the entire length of the flight." I return Mr. Brickman's greeting.

"I was sort of hoping you might have forgotten that ride in the Cub." I comment.

"Forget? I'm still having nightmares over that one.

If my memory serves me right, didn't we have engine problems with that airplane?"

"Yes, that's the one." I reply.

We both laugh as we discuss the whereabouts of the Cub that I took my Private Pilot check flight in; particularly when I tell him we still have the airplane. To add a little more color to our conversation, I mention that the airplane I brought with me is equipped with a permanently installed radio and electric starter. With that he stands and we shake hands.

After showing him my paperwork, which includes the results of a six-hour written exam, Brickman checks my logbook entry for the required spins, and the oral exam begins. Today, I must know and understand all the requirements for a Student, Private and Commercial Pilot's License, including maneuvers for each. I must verbally explain and then demonstrate each maneuver while flying from the right seat in the aircraft.

After departing Albany, we head northeast, where after about an hour into the check flight, deteriorating weather causes us to reschedule the remainder of the flight for the following week.

After completing the higher air work, we venture over to Loudon for some simulated forced landings and then stop for a short break. Don is engaged in conversation with Kenney's father Ronald Derringer. He was with the CAA prior to changing to the FAA, and is now engaged with the State Aviation Department. Both men greet Mr.Brickman and myself simultaneously as we enter the office. After shaking hands among themselves

Don dispenses four Cokes for our refreshment.

Don, tall and lean, is dressed in light tan slacks and matching open top short sleeve shirt. Convenience has him leaning against the Coke machine holding an L&M cigarette between his teeth, removing it only to sip his drink. Ron Derringer, well proportioned for his shorter stature, is wearing gray slacks, tieless white shirt and blue cap, and talks between wisps of white smoke from the pipe he holds firmly in his teeth. Brickman, the more athletically proportioned of the group, wears gray dress slacks, a white short-sleeve shirt with yellow tie, and periodically adjusts his dress hat to keep it resting properly on his head.

I now find myself witness to a very interesting impromptu conversation among three very well- known figures in our aviation community.

This conversation starts with some reminiscing of the open cockpit days, where all three started their careers. Then the conversation progresses onto the weather conditions each survived, problems encountered with the older machines, engine failures, turning farm pastures into makeshift landing strips, comparing flight training from the past to that of now, and a discussion on how the airway system has changed, including radio navigation. Even the new regulations find their way into the conversation. There is a presence that comes when reaching a certain plateau in a pilot's career. This becomes quite evident as each man speaks of flying in such a casual, nonchalant manner. I can sense the experience, confidence and passion each man has for his flying. Others who misunderstand this subject can become totally overwhelmed by the matter and never truly appreciate the fact that these men have endured what many of us have yet to experience - the test of time.

Departing Loudon, there are a few more maneuvers to perform before we travel onward to Albany. Fred prepared me well but this is, without question, the longest and most comprehensive check ride I have ever taken. After parking in the designated area at Albany, Brickman exits the left side of the airplane. Closing the right door I stand back from the wing, and watch as he stands with his back to the airplane. A moment later he turns and reaches over the back of the fuselage and shakes my hand.

"Congratulations, you are now a flight instructor."

After completing the paperwork in his office, he hands me my certificate; "Show that to Don, he can do the rest...good luck Ed."

As I walk out of the office, I have a feeling that there is more to learn, and I soon find that I am right.

More congratulations await me upon my return to home base, for today is the culmination of a lot of work. With the close of the day, we pack up the airplanes and close operations to partake in a little celebration. As I sip on a frosty cold, tasty beer, there is chatter about what rating is next, how it feels to be an instructor at 21 and of course the possibility of the airlines. I am enjoying this conversation and the great company, however, the day has taken its toll on me. I just want to go home, collect my thoughts and get some sleep. There will be other days.

The weekend is here. Don greets me as I walk through

the office door. "Are you ready to put that new instructor rating of yours to work?" My reply is immediate and full of enthusiasm. My assignment; there is a young student who is preflighting one of the Cubs; one whom Don has already instructed through his air work. It is time for his introduction to takeoffs and landings. I walk down the flight line with a purpose in my step and take time to explain our mission to my new student.

With eagerness and new found professionalism, I prop N92635 and climb into the front seat. I am about to give my first lesson in the same airplane I received my first lesson. During this flight, I find myself a little hesitant to let him go too far, as I take over the controls before a poor result is produced. The most important lesson in this flight for me is learning when to act. Because the thought crosses my mind that my student does not seem to be grasping the new maneuvers as quickly as I know he should, I decide to discuss my findings with Don. At the completion of the lesson, with a slight flourish, I make the appropriate logbook entry into the student's logbook; next to my signature I enter my certificate number, 1499344CFI. I log this flight time as dual given, another first. I later explain to Don, in what I think is intelligent technical terms, what happened during that flight. He just laughs.

"You have a certificate that states you have met the requirements for a certified flight instructor, but it does not mean you are one yet. That man you were with can learn. The question is, can you teach?" The discussion continues, and I find myself learning things that are not in the manual. I need to learn what I know; and only time will teach that to me.

"If you want to know how not to do a maneuver, ask any student. They will be glad to show you. As far as correcting mistakes, you do not know what his mistakes are until he makes them." I am soaking in this advanced education which comes with much encouragement.

That day, I am introduced to Ryan Moorhead, a corporate pilot who started with Don much the same way I did. He stands 5' 10" with straight blonde short hair, quiet spoken and very knowledgeable. During our conversation he echoes the same sentiments as Don does with regard to teaching. I make a point to ask them how they know if a student is ready for their first solo flight. I learn there is no stock answer.

Two facts are seared into my head: first, until a student has passed his or her Private Pilot Flight test, I am ultimately responsible; Second, should I solo a student in 10 flying hours, including ground time spent before and after each flight, I have less than 24 hours of time to find out what he is thinking and teach him to safely solo the airplane for at least three take-offs and landings. This is a very sobering fact.

Don explains, "the hardest part of your job will be soloing someone for the first time. Right now, do not be concerned with that. Check people out in different airplanes, finish up students for their licenses and build some time." I am beginning to see what Brickman means. The real scoop is: don't hurt anyone-don't wreck any machinery. By the end of the day, Fred, Don and Ryan all laugh when telling of their similar exploits, while, simultaneously welcoming me to " instructor hood."

After all the airplanes are put away for the night, Don leaves me with a parting comment. "Every time you get into an airplane with a student, keep one thing in mind - they have the potential of killing you. The chips are down Eddie, now the real work begins."

My beginning days as an instructor are quite busy during the weekends and summer evenings. Don and the rest of the instructors keep an eye on me as I gain experience and confidence working with the more advanced students, checking pilots out in other aircraft, and starting a few students from scratch.

I am soon engaged in not only precision with my teaching, but I find an awareness of the self-preservation that comes with the territory - I have a new found respect for my own flight instructors, not only for their professionalism and dedication but also for their courage.

I spend the better portion of my early career recovering from maneuvers of which are not found in any manual, at least not the ones I have read. In the first several months of instructing, recovering from inadvertent spins is a normal occurrence. I soon learn to allow a little more room for error, particularly with introducing new maneuvers. And the same terminology with all students does not necessarily guarantee the same results. While introducing stalls one afternoon, a student abruptly places the nose of the airplane upward and slightly beyond the vertical. My recovery includes some fast rudder work to rotate the airplane and get the nose headed for the ground to gain airspeed, all which leaves me quietly thanking Fred for his basic aerobatic instruction. Fortunately the student pays the only consequence when he swallows his gum.

Periodically between flights, I will pass Don standing in the hangar, hands on his hips, smiling and slowly nodding head.

Some days are filled with take-offs and landings; time spent saving the airplane and my own skin from disaster is as instructional as it is educational for the student.

Jim, a successful architect in his early thirties, is married with two children, and has reached the plateau where I feel he is ready for his first solo. So I discuss this possibility with Don. In his great wisdom he explains that I am the only one who can make such a decision, not even he with all his experience can call this one. I have to satisfy in my own mind my thoroughness and the student's capabilities.

It is a very calm evening when I make the decision. The session has gone well and I ask Jim to hand me his Student Pilot Certificate, which I endorse. His face expresses a little nervousness, yet at the same time it contains the excitement of anticipation for this moment. After giving some final instruction I step from the aircraft and stand alongside the runway to watch. As the airplane leaves the ground I feel like the loneliest person in the world.

I watch intently as the airplane becomes airborne and Jim flies the traffic pattern. Once the airplane is on final approach, I know the moment of truth is only seconds away, I will witness first hand the results of my work.

As the airplane is in position for a touchdown, probably due to the absence of my weight, the airplane raises slightly. Jim corrects this minor error and continues into a smooth landing on the south runway. Jim taxis the airplane over to where I am standing and I can see an enormous grin has overtaken his face. As I grasp his hand to shake, I can remember a flight instructor who stood in this same spot to congratulate me on my first solo. There is a feeling of great accomplishment, by both the student and myself.

Later, over a cold Coke, Don engages me in a conversation. Smiling he comments, "Nice job. Add a few wrinkles and some gray hair and we just might make an instructor out of you yet." A thoughtful smile is my only reaction.

Months later, I receive the opportunity to fill a full time instructor's position with a company operating out of Schenectady, New York. This will afford me more exposure and experience, something I look forward to.

Operations at Schenectady consist of a flight school, charter, and a Hughes Helicopter and Cessna dealership; all operations are conducted using newer airplanes. Management offices, operations, and large maintenance facilities are all located under one roof.

The airport has three runways, the shortest being some five thousand feet long, while the longest is 7000 feet, providing plenty of room for maneuvering. Schenectady is also home to the Air Guard, who at this time is engaged in flying KC-97's. Along with these large, four engine aircraft we also share the facilities with General Electric's corporate fleet of jets. Flying the traffic pattern requires constant vigilance due to the wake turbulence produced by the larger machine, which can be hazardous to smaller aircraft.

Among the physical changes I experience while flying out of Schenectady, there are a few business ventures to which I am totally unfamiliar, one of them is banner towing.

On this particular spring morning, Walt Grim, the president of the operation, introduces me to this segment of flying.

Walt is a friendly and confident man who walks with a definite swagger complimented by the sound of tapped heels as each shoe makes contact with the ground. Periodically a pipe and the fedora- type hat that matches his tan blazer will complete his casual dress; neither his dress nor his sense of humor distract from his professionalism.

I help with the preparation of the banner, which will later include the actual tow. The banner itself weighs approximately 20 pounds, this depending on the amount of characters. For this operation, the amount rarely exceeds 20 to 25 pounds. Each 5' x 3' nylon mesh character is assembled in the hangar and checked for proper spelling. It is then unrolled and laid out on the pavement, readable side down, and angled to the left and ahead of the takeoff path of the airplane. (20)

The tail tiedown ring on the Cessna 172 is replaced with a combination hook-release. The release is actuated by the pilot via a rope that leads up the side of the airplane and through the left window. From the head of the banner, a nylon rope line, approximately 200 feet in length is laid out and attached to the tail of the airplane. Applying half flaps and holding the brakes until full RPM is reached, the takeoff run is initiated. As the airplane nears the banner on take off, it is flown off the ground in semi-stalled flight, while literally peeling the banner off the ground, one letter at a time to insure an untangled banner.

Once airborne, a circle over the airport is necessary to allow those on the ground to check the banner for trailing legibility. The drag on the airplane produced by the banner can be equaled to dragging a large parachute. The banner, although strong for its purpose, is susceptible to tearing thus requiring much slower airspeed during flight.

The nervous part of the flight is shortly after take off when it is extremely important to keep the banner from getting tangled in the trees and possibly causing a serious accident. With the openness of Schenectady Airport, the possibility of this happening is greatly reduced. After completion of the flight, the banner is released over the airport and drops to the ground.

Barnie Gordon is our chief flight instructor: a rugged looking individual with a gift for knowing what to say, when and how. On one flight, he lost the banner when heavy turbulence severed the line attached to the banner and the banner subsequently ended up in someone's backyard. Upon his return he is summoned to the phone, and very professionally converses with the woman now in possession of our banner. Within moments he has everything smoothed over. Rubbing the back of his neck he turns and comments, "I sure hope you guys used clean words on that banner." With that we all laugh. What is not laughable, however, is that the jolt of the banner, parting company with the airplane actually leaves Barney with a stiff neck for two days.

His mannerisms and eloquence come to life again; the day the Kiwanis Club sponsors the "penny-a-pound ride". This is basically a short- sight seeing ride for sale to anyone who will subject themselves to a set of scales and pay one penny for each pound indicated. Once I heard this I approached Barnie and jokingly asked who is going to inform the female passengers their weight and who is going to collect the money. Rolling the cigarette in his mouth between his finger and thumb he smiled; "Ed my good man, watch."

The Kiwanis members, to save face, explain that the weights are necessary for their calculations; no one except us knew that the weight and balance has already been prepared for each airplane.

As the first of our passengers enter the waiting room, all eyes are on Barnie and his lovable personality, for he is one of those rare people who could tell you a joke and no one would get it.

The reactions of our passengers ranged from laughter, to red faces, to requests for a second set of scales. This continues for several minutes until one woman actually confronted Barnie and asks why her weight is so important.

With a very serious look in his face, eloquence in his voice and profound professionalism in his manner, he actually explains the process of weight and balance on the aircraft and its necessity. During this whole display, the rest of us did our best to keep smiles off our faces, wondering what the outcome might be. His success is memorable. I must say, Barney is the only one among us that could have run for political office and won.

Schenectady, as with any operation, has its share of memorable students not soon to be erased from this instructor's memory, the first to come to mind is an engineer.

Robert is not prone to successfully dividing his attentions between the required tasks both outside and inside the airplane. He will frequently become so absorbed observing other traffic in the traffic pattern that he is almost oblivious of his own actions in the airplane. Although a slight man of meek appearance, these actions approach barbarism when operating the controls of the airplane.

The wisps of hair over his forehead soon are dampened with perspiration while his glasses hang precariously on the edge of his nose. He abruptly pulls the carburetor heat control on and closes the throttle to idle. Then he reacts by abruptly reversing his actions which only compound his first mistake, which he will repeat. The events are happening so fast that neither the needle of the tachometer nor I can keep up with actions. After several unsuccessful attempts to slow his movements, he reaches for the carb heat control handle, pulling it so hard that the cable becomes disconnected at the carburetor. Holding the control handle in his hand, he examines the almost three feet of cable attached to it, then looks up at me for my reaction. With a certain amount of displeasure in my voice I ask, "Now how do we propose to fix that?"

With a very sheepish grin on his face, he adjusts his glasses and inch-by-inch starts feeding the cable back into the control panel.

Another memorable student if mine is Neil, a student of aeronautics attending one of the local colleges. Neil and I are scheduled to fly to Kingston, New York, on his second cross-country flight. The previous nights weather system has moved through leaving us with high surface winds and heavy turbulence. The flight Service Station informs me of several pilot reports of heavy turbulence along our route of flight, one of them being from an American Airlines four-engine turbo-prop, hence the training flight is rescheduled.

Without calling beforehand, Neil arrives for his flight and I explain the situation. Standing before me, dressed in his ski sweater and pressed slacks, he engages in a rather elaborate explanation about turbulence, how can I, a flight instructor not know about rising air and its effect on an aircraft? Be it a large or small airplane, the mass of air has the same effect... realizing there are no words to stop this conversation, I interrupt him; "OK, get in the airplane".

He fairs rather well until we are just north of Kingston, whereby one look at his face made me realize the turbulence is having an effect.

"Concentrate on flying and navigating, we are almost there, you will be alright." After landing, he excuses himself, and a few moments later I find him next to the coke machine, where he just finished chugging down a cold soda. I explain to him it would have been better to drink water before the return flight.

"That's OK, I know all about these things." He replies.

I reply; "oooh kay!"

Fifteen minutes after departing Kinston, the inevitable happened. Before I can reach for a "sic sac", Neil places his head out of the window he so hurriedly opens and parts company with his coke - into the propeller slipstream. He turns around with one sorry looking face.

"Neil! Are you ok?" Before I can react, it is evident we are in for an instant replay so I grab him by the back of the neck and hold his head out toward the rear of the window to allow the waste to go with the slipstream, while at the same time trying to keep the airplane straight and level. This is repeated twice more before returning to Schenectady. Upon our arrival, the aircraft is placed in maintenance where it takes two hours to clean. I wait for Neil to exit the rest room whereupon I confront him and inquire about his physical well – being. His reply; "You were right about that coke."

Veronica is a loveable grandmother and registered nurse, and although not mechanically inclined nor in possession of great inherent coordination, she is a woman of great determination and curiosity. Her idea for departing the ramp is accomplished by applying almost full power before she releases the brakes. This is followed by my rapid maneuvering to prevent a collision with the fuel truck that the lineman has taken refuge behind, an action to which she will comment on how fast the lineman can run.

Her fascination with the control tower while taxiing past usually ends with the airplane headed right for it which requires turning off the engine, removing the tow bar from the airplane and manually pushing the machine back onto the main taxiway. During this time she sits in the airplane explaining how much easier it would be if I just use reverse.

Trimming the airplane for level flight she holds the control wheel while applying full nose down trim. A screech is released from her mouth upon releasing her grip on the control wheel as the nose abruptly heads for the ground.

Stall recoveries usually end up in a spin or half inverted to which she insisted there is something wrong with this airplane. She feels I should pick out a better one for her next lesson.

One afternoon, after completion of another lesson, she explains to me that her interest in flying has waned and hoped I would not be offended with her decision to stop flying, "Would you like to know what I am going to try next?"

I answer, a hearty "no." With that she gives me a big hug and departs.

Not all of the interesting experiences include the actual flying of an airplane, which I learn toward the end of the summer when a Cessna representative approaches us with his campaign for introducing the new 172; bring the airplane to the public, place it inside malls, large stores, meeting rooms and halls even if this means complete disassembly and reassembly. We find this idea intriguing, and after a few days of discussion, it is decided to place the airplane inside the large banquet room of one of the most prestigious banquet clubs in the area. After dismantling, the aircraft is taken by truck to the banquet club and reassembled.

Access to this room is at the bottom of an elaborate stairway that leads to a very exotic bar located on a mezzanine. The very elegant doors to the room are not opened to the public until cocktail hour on opening night.

When the doors are officially opened to reveal the airplane, Barnie and I are seated in the mezzanine to witness the initial reactions. At first, curiosity blends with disbelief. Then, the verbal response gains momentum, "What's that?"

"It's an airplane!"

"How did it get here?"

This verbal exchange becomes the focal point of great curiosity attracting the entire club, including the wedding party from another banquet room. The entire event made for very memorable summer champagne.

The fall arrives, and brings with it new regulations regarding flight instructor ratings. The emphasis is on updating all instructors to regulation changes and standardization of all maneuvers required for each flight test. Until now, an instructor's rating was good for life. Under the new regulations, each flight instructor must renew his/her certificate every 24 calendar months.

To qualify for this renewal, during this time period each flight instructor is required to graduate at least ten students who have passed their appropriate flight test on the first attempt. If this criterion is not met, a flight check and/or oral exam may be required for recertification.

Most local instructors and many from surrounding states arrive for three days of ground schooling and flight checks. Many of these instructors have been instructing before I began flying, some had been flying before I was born. Today we have one common denominator - we must renew and upgrade all our certificates.

Throughout this time period, my studies continue toward an instrument rating. I study new navigational charts that depict airways and radio stations. There are no rivers, valleys or roads to use for navigational reference points. Only airports with instrument approaches are listed along with corresponding approach plates. There are new regulations for minimum and maximum altitudes, and amount of fuel to be carried for each flight, planned alternate airports holding patterns and emergency radio procedures. Finally pilots must learn a new language and short hand for copying clearances to comply with each route of flight.

Once again Fred is my mentor and again he raises the bar until the results of his teaching are demonstrated in my performance. From take-off to just a few hundred feet above the ground at our destination, Fred has me fly the entire trip solely with reference to instruments. The day of my flight check is positive proof of his teaching; I am the only one of five applicants in that week who receives his instrument rating.

Later that day, in a discussion with Fred, it is suggested that an Instrument Flight Instructors Rating would be the next reasonable step toward my career goals; so it is done, as is my return to Loudon on a full - time basis.

Fred informs me of the status of two mutual acquaintances and former students of his who are now flying for Northeast Airlines, both having finished their probationary period and now received their permanent assignments. The airline is accepting applications for possible future hires, and it is suggested that I make a flight over to Logan Airport in Boston, Massachusetts to introduce myself in person and fill out an application. A pilot flying in to talk to the flight department not only makes a good impression but it can lead to a brief interview and placement on an active list. With this information, I borrow an airplane and fly into Logan to make my presence known.

My arrival is quite timely; although there are no immediate plans for a new class, I am asked to periodically update my application, with particular interest in any future ratings and total flying time. Although there are more requirements to fulfill, the incentive is positive.

On the return flight, I deviate just north of course and take time to locate Colrain, MA. By following what I can see of the roads through the foliage, I am able to fairly well establish myself over the site, where several years ago Dave Wallace was found. I am studying the thick wooded area and realize that there is no way anyone could have seen his craft from the air. As I circle, I remember his encouragement and prodding for me to earn my ratings; he would stand before me with his arms folded over his chest and glasses resting on top of his forehead, "get on with it."

With a thumb up gesture, I level the wings and pick up a new heading for home while wondering what his reaction to this flight might have been.

Over the next few years there were similar flights and visits to Boston, each time updating my total flying time and ratings. The time arrived when my qualifications matched the requirements as a new class was being started. Word had been forwarded to me I would receive a telegram within seven to ten days. On the day the telegrams were being prepared, a financial situation was the cause for the last minute cancellation of the new class.

Chapter Seven

The Seasoning

To the right of the final approach to Loudon's south runway, is the old familiar weathervane casting its last shadow for the day in the setting summer sun. After the students have left for the day, Harold Green, the newest member of our instructional staff, stands in the office searching all his pockets. He is looking for the notes listing the students he has flown today, so that he can transfer this information to his logbook. He stands 5'4" with dark complexion, and short black hair, and chuckles while commenting on each found note, "Here's one. Yup. There's another, both these guys have a way to go; this one just won't listen to reason."

I ask Harold, " What do you do with that one?"

"I give him a reason to listen."

Don, Ted, and shortly after Fred and myself join him. One by one we look at our respective notes, making comments on the events of that flight. The exchanging of stories continues for some time; Ted mentions one of his students who retracts the flaps too soon after takeoff, "That might just put a guy in the trees in a hurry!" Ted comments.

Then Harold starts, "Didn't someone trim the hedgerow on the approach end of the north runway last week?" Everyone looks at me. I had a student, whose improper use of the flaps caused them to retract prematurely on final approach, which would have landed us short of the runway. In that instance, I was able to keep the airplane from hitting the ground, but not quick enough to stop a fast trimming of the hedgerow. As a souvenir I gave the student one of the branches.

Then Don adds, "Look at this. This one's idea of full flap stall recovery ends up in a spin."

"Ya know that darn machine wants to recover inverted until you dump the flaps!" Don comments.

Then it was Fred's turn, "This one, every time I put the hood on him, he closes his eyes. I almost think he does better that way." To us a good laugh is a great way to end the day.

We are not the only ones happy to see summer arrive that year; Carl Reinko, a local aircraft owner, had complained all spring because his wife would not let him fly his Cessna 150. Some birds had built a nest in the engine compartment and until they were all hatched and flown away, he was not to disturb the nest.

The day starts out hot, hazy and humid. Even without a forecast we know what to expect before the day is over. About 3:30, the expected happened. Thunderstorms start moving down what is called thunderstorm alley, in advance of a cold front (21). The blackened sky gives the lightning flashes a closer appearance than normal, and one by one we head for home and the tie downs.

Ted is taxiing the 172 into the hangar; Don and his student are behind me, running as fast as my student. Then there is me, but I'm not as fast as Fred and his student who has beaten all of us inside the hangar where Harold greets us, "It sure is heartening knowing the Loudon Airport Instructors know enough to come in out of the rain."

After we gather inside the hangar, the sound of the rain on the metal roof is so loud we visually check to see if it has turned to hail. We then enter the office and close the door to deaden the sound, whereby one by one we search for change to use in the coke machine.

There is a very loud bang. Startled, I can almost feel the hair on the back of my neck stand on end as the lights go out. The hangar has taken a lightning strike. While in the darkness someone mentions the smell of smoke. A moment later the lights come back on and we see that the radio on the metal cabinet used for airport advisories is consumed in smoke.

The ringing of the phone is barely audible above the sound of the rain. Ted answers it. Motioning for Don to take the call he says in a louder than normal voice, "Wait until you hear this one!" It is still raining hard when Don exits the phone booth; it seems the caller was quite upset when Don explained that due to the weather we could not fly him to Syracuse, N.Y. In an attempt to change Don's mind, the caller told of a movie he had once seen about an old charter pilot with the small airplane who always gets through the worst weather no matter what. We all laughed as the lights went out again, and in the darkness we hear, "What is the name of the movie?"

In a louder voice Don asks, "What?"

The question is repeated.

"Why?"

The answer; "I want to see it!"

After the rain subsides, we all pitch in to secure operations for the day. Walking out the door, Harold turns to Don and asks, "Well?" Don looks at him inquisitively. "What was the name of the movie?"

There is a more realistic and serious side to their flying, which is expressed when engaged in their work. Each individual personality is unique as is their share of both good flights and those not so graced. On rare occasions, where tragedy has been averted, the discussion involving the events is interesting to witness. This might be accompanied by a slight shaking of the head, or barely audible profanity. Rarely will the participant take full, yet well-deserved credit for the outcome; instead the credit will be given to great fortune, or luck.

My logbook now shows almost two thousand hours and although still the youngest of the group, my peers consider me an equal. It is more than just hours in a logbook that make a pilot, it is a metamorphasis whose end result can be seen in mannerisms, speech and most importantly in flying skills; it is commonly referred to as "the seasoning". I will begin to understand this a little more clearly on a cold February morning.

John Frederick, a retired fighter pilot, is finishing his recurrency check with me in one of our Cessna 150's. N8608G: it is the only 150 available on the schedule this day and the only 150 on the field equipped with extended range tanks. We take advantage of the west-northwest surface wind blowing diagonally across the airport as we alternate using the north and the west runway for crosswind landings.

Proceeding to Albany, the traffic for runway 28 is considerably heavier than normal. As a result, our clearances from the tower are wider and are time consuming patterns. Although a great exercise in radio communications and traffic control, this technique also results in fewer landings. Due to these conditions, I decide to depart for Schenectady before returning to home base.

During the ten-mile flight to Schenectady, I am enjoying a conversation with John while comparing the radio procedures for Albany and Schenectady. Approaching Schenectady, the tower clears us to runway 22; a concrete runway 7,000 feet long which, to our delight, has little traffic today. John very professionally reports our location over the Knolls Atomic Power Plant prior to entering the traffic pattern.

Encounters with turbulence today are few and far and few between and the airplane is performing well in the cold, cloudless sky. I find myself totally self-indulged, with little thought of anything save the ordinary to earmark today's flight. After a very nice touchdown, John retracts the flaps, adds power and proceeds with the touch-and- go landing.

After gaining approximately 150, feet we encounter a sudden change of plans- the engine falters, a spurt of power, then it ceases to function. I can feel the airplane slow down as I immediately take over the controls, "Woaahh, I got it John!" I push forward on the control wheel to lower the nose to maintain airspeed, while simultaneously checking for enough clear runway for an emergency landing. I am also operating the carburetor heat, changing the throttle position, and switching the ignition from one magneto to the other in an attempt restore power. I am performing all of this while at the same time completing a dead stick landing.

This happens so fast that there is not enough time for me to even get nervous. As I notify the tower of our predicament on the roll out, I am greeted with yet another surprise; the propeller is still turning. I advance the throttle and the RPM's increase; I cannot believe my senses. John and I start questioning each other, hoping neither one of us has lost our "faculties."

I request a clearance off the active runway at the intersection of runways 22 and 28, which is just about two hundred feet from the end of the longest runway in the area. My request is granted along with some chuckling from Dick in the tower. This whole thing must look like I am simulating it at the last moment to test everyone's reaction. One thing is certain, our reactions in the airplane have certainly been tested. Once parked on the intersecting runway, I performed the complete pre-take-off checklist; everything is within limits.

I do not have an answer for what just happened. Thus, my frustration is soon replaced with inquiry and doubt. I keep asking myself: "was there anything I did or could have done to cause/prevent this?"

I am left with one alternative.

I call the tower to request clearance back up runway 22 for another take-off. I will try this again, knowing ahead of time that I have enough room in case of duplication.

Then I ask myself, "duplication of what?"

Taxiing back for take-off I am the recipient of a little jesting from my friend in the tower as he chuckles over the mic. So in turn I follow suit. I start asking myself more questions, "How far do I taxi down the runway? What if there is nothing wrong with this airplane? If there is something wrong, will it happen at the same place?"

I find myself frustrated and a little apprehensive as I approach a point to initiate a take-off.

With conviction I apply full throttle and proceed with a normal take-off. At approximately 130 feet, all of my questions are answered. Without any apology at all, the engine falters and quits. I now have an exact duplication of the previous take-off, including restoration of power on the landing roll. I inform the tower of our condition and after receiving a clearance to the ramp, I am actually able to taxi the airplane under its own power. Unfastening my belt I look at John, "John, you still with me?" He just smiles and nods his head.

Once inside operations, I ask for Dick Derringer, who is head of maintenance, and explain my situation. He arrives at the airplane, opens the access door on the cowling and pulls the fuel quick drain release to see if there's a fuel feed to the engine. He questions me about the amount of fuel on board. I explain to him at the time of departure from Loudon, there was enough fuel onboard for four hours of flight.

"When the engine quit it sounded like either fuel or air starvation." After working up enough nerve to tell him that it had happened twice, he asks me why and I reply by asking him what he would have done under the same circumstances. He shakes his head and suggests I try it again, this time alone.

So I do, this time on runway 28. If there was ever a time I wanted an engine to quit, this moment is it. I make the take-off, climb to 150 feet, then land the airplane without incident. I return to the ramp where we all stand shaking our heads. At this point I call home base and inform Don of our predicament.

He first asks if we are all right. Next he wants to know how bad the airplane is damaged.

"It's not. The airplane is OK. I was able to get on the runway without incident other than no power." I leave it at that. I will wait for a more appropriate time to inform him that I had just had two forced landings. That is, provided there is such a time.

After he arrives at Schenectady, Don immediately starts inspecting 08G, while asking me questions as to what the engine sounded like. To his questions I reply with the same answers I had already given to Dick. At this point, I find myself questioning everything I know about airplanes, considering the fact that this machine quit twice, then operated perfectly on the third try.

"Twice, why twice?" He looks at me as if I have four heads; I am not surprised by his reaction and again explain the whole scenario. He casually replies, "Oh."

Now Don is going to give it a try. If it continues to run he will gain altitude over the airport and try for home, if not, we will leave the airplane here and return home in the 172.

Without incident, the airplane is flown home. I follow in the 172. Upon our arrival, John and I verbally follow every step of our flight trying to find an answer, so much so that by this time we have questioned our moves so many times it is ridiculous.

According to Don there is only one way to find the answer; dismantle the fuel system. I am directed to remove the upper wing panels that cover the tanks while Don removes the engine cowling to check the system forward of the firewall. I felt guilty for having this machine grounded - it should be in the air where it belongs. However I realize it is better to have the machine here in the hangar where we can work on it instead of being scattered over some piece of real estate.

Each quick drain is removed from the bottom of each tank, all the fuel is removed and inspected and later disposed of. Don removes the fuel system forward of the firewall including the engine fuel sump drain - there are no obstructions or contaminations to be found. The air intake and the carburetor are removed and inspected with the same results.

The wing panels on top of the wing provide another challenge. They have not been touched since the airplane was built three years before. The hangar and the metal are cold, and scraping a few knuckles does not improve my disposition.

At the end of the second day, I have removed the wing panel exposing the tank for the right wing, and it is decided to wait until tomorrow for the actual removal of the wing tank before proceeding to the left side. As we are closing the shop for the day, John stops by to inquire of our progress. We still do not have an answer, which only adds to my frustration.

The next morning finds me in the hangar looking at the airplane in its state of partial disassembly,which has exposed its most intimate workings. Preparing for the day's work, I almost feel sad for this piece of metal that can't speak on it's own behalf. A few moments later, Don arrives and proceeds to crawl underneath the airplane. Using a screwdriver and a wrench, he removes a small plate from the belly of the airplane. Using a shop light he inspects the standpipe, which is part of the fuel system.

"They say airplanes don't lie, that if you look hard enough they will tell you everything." I can feel a questionable look come over my face.

The fuel is gravity fed to the engine from the two tanks in the wings. At the low point of each tank is a sump and quick drain; here a sampler is used to check for contaminants in the tank. The fuel lines, one for each tank, are located inside the fuselage walls and lead down to a manually operated fuel shutoff that is located on the floor between the student and the instructor. This valve is located at a "T" in the system. From there it is fed to the engine compartment where it goes through another fuel sump with a drain. This allows the pilot to sample the fuel from the tanks to the engine, again to catch any contaminants.

At the "T", where the fuel shutoff valve is located, there is a standpipe. This runs vertically from the shut off valve on the floor to a plate on the exterior belly of the airplane. This is also a catchall. According to the manufacturer, this part of the fuel system does not have a quick drain; requiring exposure and draining only during the annual inspection of the airplane.

"Eddie, let's get the salamander and heat this up just a little bit."

After about a minute, Don pulls out a piece of ice from the standpipe, about the size of a small pencil, with a rounded eraser. As we examine the evidence, the story unfolds.

I closely follow each hand gesture and mental picture Don is making. As moisture builds up in the system from condensation, what cannot be drained out at each location collects in the standpipe. So long as we are doing take offs and landings at the rate we were at Loudon, the moisture really had not had the chance to freeze. Our flight to Albany and the short time between take-off and landings coupled with the heat on the floor was just enough to prevent the moisture from freezing to the point that its expansion would block the flow of fuel to the engine.

Don narrates, "On your way to Schenectady, there was enough time in level flight attitude and at cold enough temperatures, that the moisture started to set. Fortunately, there was not enough ice to completely block off the fuel flow in the line the standpipe was connected to. On your approach, with reduced power and nose low attitude, the fuel actually squeezed over the top of the moisture, which had frozen all the way up the standpipe forming a crown, which only partially blocked the fuel line."

"As you rotated on take off, there was enough ice on the top of the standpipe to prevent any fuel flow to the engine, leaving only fuel in the line from the shutoff valve to the engine; at that point the engine quit. Once back on the ground in a level attitude, enough fuel passed over the partial obstruction enabling the engine to continue running. The second take-off was the same as the first. The airplane sat while you were trying to figure out what happened, the heat left in the cabin melted some of the ice. When Dick pulled the drain on the engine sump there was a steady stream and probably drained some of the moisture out allowing for an uneventful flight home. That is the reason why it flew fine for me on the way home."

I ask Don where he found this information, he directed me to the office and the morning mail. I pick up a postcard from the FAA. It is a recent AD note. (Airworthiness Directive) (22). The message is rather short and to the point: *On Cessna 150's with extended range tanks, the standpipes should be drained free of moisture at intervals of 100 hours flying time in lieu of annual inspection, or whichever comes first. With noncompliance, engine stoppage might be experienced.* I place the postcard back on the desk.

Returning to the shop where Don is reassembling 08G, he decides that for what little effort is required to perform this, it will be done at each oil change, or twentyfive hours flying time.

That evening, while making some entries in my own logbook, I cannot help but think about the circumstances as they were played out. If the engine quit at Loudon, I would no doubt have ended up in a snow covered field or some tree. At Albany, chances were a little better, even with our flight pattern changed as many times as it was. Then, there was Schenectady: the longest runway in the area, with little traffic to speak of. I decided to be thankful for the way things turned out, and I hoped that the incidences that led to this AD note ended as well as mine. I place a small #1 and #2 in the remarks column to record two engine failures in one day, hoping they will be the last.

For the last two years, we have been plagued with rumors about the airport becoming an industrial park. Unfortunately, as spring draws closer, we are informed that the industrial park is a definite; the airport is not. Although disappointed, we are not surprised.

The news travels fast; one of the most popular and respected operations in the area is about to end. We are not looking for anyone's sympathy we are merely looking for answers. Where does one put an airport? Other locations such as Mechanicville, Albany, Round Lake and even Columbia County are being considered, including a proposal to move the operation to Poestenkill, just outside of Troy, N.Y. A difficult decision, to say the least, is solely upon the shoulders of one man if the business is to continue.

On a quiet spring afternoon, we are all gathered in the office. After several rings Don enters the phone booth, listens for a moment, and then hangs up the receiver. The property has been sold. The airport is closed.

The decision is made to move to Poestenkill, and by the following week the move is already under way. Considering the circumstances our spirits are high. With only 500 feet of the runway useable due to mud, our move is quite interesting. The move also includes the maiden flight of Richard's rebuilt Navion. The remainder of the weekend finds us shuttling all the airplanes to our new home, which includes a 2800-foot north-south gravel runway with hills on both approaches and a mountain ridge to the east.

Several days are spent removing and relocating tie down rings, ropes and other equipment necessary for our operation. We keep ourselves busy, but there is something missing. It is even noticeable among the instructors as their conversations are relatively bland and lacking in enthusiasm.

After all the equipment has been relocated, Don and I fly the 8608G over to the site of the old airport to pick up the only Cub left of the fleet. Approaching downwind for the south runway, the old familiar windsock stands majestically confirming my choice of runways. Aligning with that runway, I remember the day I made my first solo to this same runway; today, I make a final approach for another reason.

After landing, we survey the barren grounds; all tie down rings and ropes have been removed. As we enter the office, there is an eerie emptiness; void of furniture, the phone booth the coke machine, and most importantly void of the camaraderie of the pilots that gave life to this room.

In the shop, all tools and materials have been relocated to their new location. I notice a familiar poster on the wall; it is an old remnant illustrating the repair of Plexiglas canopies on WW II aircraft. I remember asking Don about this the day I started to work here. I carefully remove it for safekeeping. Walking across the hangar floor our footsteps echo in the emptiness, as I double-check the hangar doors that have been closed for the last time. Since our landing, not a word has been spoken, for our actions speak loudly of the sadness we both share.

Don has readied the Cub, which I prop for him. As he taxis to the runway I follow behind on foot up to the point where he stops for a mag check. It is here where he takes one more look at the old hangar. Closing the Cub door, he continues taxiing northbound until there is sufficient runway for take off. No matter where a pilot is, or what he is doing; he will always stop to witness another take off. Today, not unlike others, I witness 92635 lift off and head for her new home.

I glance once again at the old hangar, remembering the people and events so vividly I can almost see them at the open hangar doors waving goodbye. I walked through those old hangar doors many times as a kid eagerly looking forward to my chores, whatever they might have been, just happy to be near an airplane. I remember the mechanics, pilots and instructors, who bolstered my high hopes and instilled realistic values in me.

There is now an eerie silence about the airport, as if in preparation of her funeral. Standing at the end of the taxiway, I feel a lump in my throat as I pay my last respects to a grand old lady.

Turning around for a last look at Bald Mountain to the east, I witness the windsock embrace a slight gust of wind with flawless conviction. This place will always be a part of me, and for that reason alone she will never die. She raised many pilots and stood for many things, and I know what was learned here will never be forgotten.

As I walk to the airplane, I search for an appropriate farewell. I turn toward the hangar one last time; with a smile on my face I hold out my hand and give a "Thumbs Up".

On April 4, 1968, I make the last official departure from Loudon Airport (23).

126

Chapter Eight

The Devil's Cape

The 2800-foot north-south gravel runway sits in a bowl, relative to the surrounding terrain. A large hill, supporting a road and power lines occupies the south end, while the north end has it's own challenge. Once clear of the power lines and tall trees there is yet another hill, whose incline almost matches the climb rate of our aircraft. The initial departure path in this direction takes us over a residential area near rooftop level. Beyond that, the hill falls away rapidly to expose a large farm affording considerably more air between airplane and obstructions.

To the west of the runway, tall trees mark the edge of the swamp that the airport is built on. To the east is a ridge some call a mountain, others a hill - by any definition it must be dealt with, particularly during high wind conditions, low visibility and nighttime operations.

After securing the aircraft for the evening, Ted, Don, Dave Carling (the operator of Poestenkill), and I, occupy a few chairs while discussing the attributes of our new location. Dave is a big man, standing six foot tall, 225 pounds, with dark hair. As he engages in conversation, he holds his right hand upward and slightly closed, while moving this hand side to side. His facial expression discloses a fish-eyed look, as though he were looking right through you. His background includes thousands of hours in large multi-engine aircraft. Presently he flies a company owned twin-engine aircraft based at Poestenkill.

Dave's trips in the company Twin Comanche are primarily for relocating personnel, or for carrying light cargo from one site to another. The airplane is rarely operated with more than two passengers at one time, thus affording me the opportunity to ride as a co-pilot and receive some multi-engine flight experience. I engage in a new type of flying that brings with it the addition of another rating, and a new column in my logbook; a column that will prove to be as interesting as any other.

Flying into major airports as JFK, LaGuardia and Newark are the beginnings of my exposure to this type of flying; an exposure that will greatly increase with the arrival of a new Turbo Charged Twin Comanche (24).

Although somewhat smaller then most light twins, its sleek design and color scheme are the object of much attention. The aircraft is painted white with black and gold trim. The wing tip tanks that provide extra range are of matching colors. The interior hosts maroon leather seats with matching carpet and a built-in oxygen system. Although equipped to carry six, the two small rear seats limit four as a more realistic capacity.

The physical layout of the instruments is just as impressive, and conforms to the new standardization for easier monitoring during flight. The engine instruments are just as impressive, and easily readable from the pilots seat. There are the throttles, propeller and mixture control handles, each color-coded and shaped for easy recognition. At the bottom of the engine control pedestal are two vernier controls for the manual operation of each turbo charger, with the cowl flap controls below these.

The latest in electronics grace the center of the instrument panel, enabling the airplane to be flown virtually anywhere under instrument flight conditions, including ILS approaches. Added to this complement of radios is a transponder, a devise that permits radar detection even in the heaviest of precipitation; high on an instrument pilot's wish list.

A few days later, I have the opportunity to fly as co-pilot to Saranac Lake and deliver two passengers to a company job site. Departing from Albany, I start the procedural radio sequence of frequencies for taxiing, clearance and departure. The 100 nautical-mile airway from Albany to Saranac Lake is labeled Victor 3; our clearance is for 8,000 feet. Once airborne, we are issued a frequency from Boston Center, the controlling agency for our flight.

Once at altitude, I begin making mental notes of the performance figures for this airplane. Turbos, having been manually operated, afford us sea level power at altitude; 27 inches Manifold Pressure, RPM 2400, fuel flow 9.5 gallons per hour per engine. At this rate, with the tip tanks, we have five hours of fuel on board. The real joy is our true airspeed - 225 mph.

Approaching the second half of our flight, I notice the rain and turbulence increasing in intensity. At one point, the clouds become so thick that the wing tip tanks are no longer visible. I hear a controller from Boston advising two airliners with heading changes to avoid some weather depicted on his radar screen near the Saranac area. It is at this point that I inquire as to our location with regards to this depicted weather. The response is almost sarcastic. "You're right in the middle of it." I realize that it is senseless to ask for radar vectors around something we are already half way through.

There is a sudden hard jolt as the airplane hits a rising wall of air, the force pushes me so hard into my seat I can barely raise my arms. Dave has disengaged the autopilot and has reduced power; the sudden onslaught of the heavy rain is so loud I can hardly hear myself think. The airplane stops as suddenly as it started up and reverses direction. I think for a moment that my seatbelt would tear into me in its determined effort to confine my body to the seat. Each time the airplane hits another wall of moving air the shock mounted instrument panel shakes so hard I am convinced that something will break. I find it astounding to think that any engine can continue to perform under such conditions, then quickly put this thought out of my mind. What seems to be an eternity, in actuality, takes only minutes. It ends as abruptly as it starts.

Judging by the look on Dave's face, he has mastered the art of extinguishing fright quickly, and returns to the matters at hand. I am slower to respond, as I catch my breath and wipe the excess moisture from my hands onto my slacks. The passengers, although not completely calm, trust their well-being to Dave and me, as one of them comments on the ride while trying to light a cigarette with a hand that refuses to be steady. Looking out the left side of the airplane Dave and I witness a flashing of light from a nearby cloud. It is at this time Boston Center calls us to inquire about the flight conditions we have just encountered.

General Aviation is not well liked by all; this is usually expressed by mocking the size of the airplanes we fly and for the most part is generally taken with a grain of salt. However, I cannot help but feel almost hostile toward anyone who does not inform all aircraft of such conditions. Unfortunately, I am not able to stand before this individual to express my thoughts. The tone of the voice heard over the radio seems more condescending than inquisitive. Regaining as much composure as fast as possible, I return the centers call, with a report of moderate turbulence and light rain. This, of course, is purely retaliatory in its content.

I return my interest to the navigation mode of the autopilot. It will actually correct for heading changes while navigating on the airway, and is installed in many of these light twins as an extra pair of hands. On the return trip home at 9,000 feet, the weather is considerably better as the setting sun gives way to a star studded-sky. The steady drone of the engines is pleasing to the ears as I look through the open veins on the engine cowling just ahead of the leading edge of the wing; there I can see the red-orange color of the turbo charger.

Heavy equipment, as employed by the airlines and corporate flight departments not only incorporates the best in electronic devices, but also are flown by two pilots. A fact that is rarely addressed or understood by our opponents is that the greatest majority of these light twins flying, even in this type of weather, are single pilot operations.

The only FAA requirement for two pilots is in an aircraft having a maximum gross weight 12,500 pounds or more. Why the workload in an airplane that weighs less has different regulations has always been questionable. Talk to any pilot whose flight consists of flying in weather single pilot in a twin, and he will gladly explain this complete fallacy in the explicit vernacular of the street. This type of flying leaves little room for error and in some cases has been a contributing factor in accidents.

The weather briefing discloses rain, showers and IFR conditions along our route of flight, which will take us to Pittsburgh, Flint Michigan and return us home via Saranac Lake; the only place where the weather is forecasted to be clear all day. Except for the return leg to Albany, I will occupy the left seat.

Departing Albany, we climb to 10,000 feet which barely put us on top of the cloud layer for the leg to Pittsburgh. Upon our arrival, the weather is reported as 500 overcast and 2 miles. Due to the low ceiling and visibility, all aircraft will be required to fly the more precise ILS approach.

Departing Pittsburgh through a rainy cloud layer, we are once again on top at 10,000 feet. The weather at Flint is not much different than Pittsburgh and requires another ILS. The landing on runway nine at Bishop International is quite normal. On my next visit, however, this airport will look a lot different and the landing not so uneventful.

Even though the Twin Commanche is a derivative of the single engine version, it is not as docile on landings, nor as forgiving as its forerunner. Despite its impressive performance, it is not prone to carrying the payload of its larger brothers, nor does it have the ice carrying capability.

Departing Flint, once again our clearance altitude places us on top of the overcast. Here we request to continue under visual flight rules at an altitude of 13,500 feet, direct to Saranac Lake, New York and monitor the different frequencies on the way.

On this leg of the trip I am instructed in the use of the oxygen system. After passing 10,000 feet, Dave adjusts his oxygen mask and directs me to wait before I do the same. Under his instruction, I actually experience the first sensations of hypoxia. This is an on demand-oxygen system, and can administer oxygen only when the user inhales. My first reaction, after placing the oxygen mask on my face, is to breathe in as much oxygen as quickly as possible. However, too much oxygen can lead to the opposite, or hyperventilation, from doing exactly that.

Approaching Saranac Lake, the weather is as forecasted and the best we have seen all day; clear skies, good visibility. To the south we can see the cloud deck that extends up to 30 miles south of our position confirming earlier forecasts of less than perfect weather at Albany.

Because we are reaching lower altitudes the oxygen masks are stored, turbos disengaged, and there is a surprise for me. Dave has turned off all radios in the airplane and announces that we will be landing on a highway that the company is building. Due to blasting, all transmitters must be turned off. Smiling, Dave looks at me and asks, while pointing over my shoulder, "How would you like to land this thing on that road?" Looking at the site, there seems more than enough room, thus I acknowledge his question with an affirmative answer.

With his usual tongue in cheek and fish-eyed look he remarks, "Another smart allecky kid." His offer to give the landing to me was just a tease.

I smile as I observe his landing on a freshly paved, unmarked highway. After our arrival, I comment on his decision to land the airplane considering the fact that this road is better than our own runway. To this we both laugh. Before departing I am able to phone Saranac Lake Flight Service for a briefing and flight plan. Albany is reporting 900 feet overcast and 2 miles in light rain; not that bad, but not great.

Dave and I agree that after returning home a nice steak will be the prefect ending to our day. With Dave in the left seat, we depart from our make-shift runway at sunset, while I tune to the FSS frequency. It has been a long day; steak or not I just want to sit in a seat that doesn't move. After copying our clearance and changing to Boston Center, I reach down for the appropriate enroute chart for the last and shortest leg home.

As I prepare for the instrument portion of our flight, the red warning light for the right turbo flashes on, "Dave, we got a light!"

At first it is thought that the turbo itself has become inoperative and the flight will have to be made without the assistance of turbo chargers. I glance outside to ensure that we are still in the clear. When I look up again the oil pressure gauge drops rapidly, and oil temperature rises simultaneously with the surging of the right propeller following this. We are definitely losing the right engine.

To my left, I witness Dave rapidly pulling the right throttle to the closed position, corresponding propeller control to the full feather position and mixture control to idle cut off; this is accomplished in a matter of seconds. There is a vibration and yawing of the airplane as the leading edge of both blades is turned forward and the right propeller is feathered and rendered motionless. As we prepare ourselves for single engine operations, I suddenly get an uneasy feeling about the integrity of the operating engine.

The passengers in the back seat are obviously nervous, as indicated by their facial expressions. It does not take a PhD to see that one of these propellers is not turning. I inform Boston of our predicament; in the controllers reply the tone of his voice is almost questioning the accuracy of my statement as he inquires about the deposition of our flight plan.

All this is happening at once, with everyone looking to us for a reason why that engine quit when it did. The passengers are expressing their concerns about our arrival at Albany; after all, we are the pilots, and don't we know that busy people have better things to do? I feel some pity for these passengers, for in their own way they are expressing their ignorance. Up to this point, they have not seen any real danger, their bodies are still in one piece thanks to a pilot who understands single engine operations. My pity grows, as I understand that even if I had the time to fully explain how and why this airplane is still able to fly, they would actually choose to remain ignorant.

Boston center again inquires as to our intentions. As Dave and I are assessing the situation I again reply to Boston "stand by". There is one known fact; neither Dave nor I are overly enthusiastic about flying into deteriorating conditions on one engine.

When a problem exists, the pilot outwardly may appear calm compared to those who do not understand the situation. This is due in part to the fact that the machine has his undivided attention. Interestingly enough, in the operations manual of any aircraft, there is a section on emergency procedures and explicit instructions for any given circumstance. Each procedure is written down in chronological order, how to accomplish each in a very tidy manner, and what to do in case none of the above works.

Someone who has given all options considerable thought put this in writing. Whoever the author, he might sit at a desk with a cup of coffee and digest what has been written, possibly analyzing each move. Should he not be satisfied with the procedures, he can stop his work to think things over. The outcome not only looks good on paper, the vocabulary is printable.

As with our passengers and controller, none of the above is responsible for the consequences of their actions should the outcome be negative; however, the author might take credit if all the procedures work as written. Where the pilot is concerned, if the procedure fails, it is deemed pilot error; if it works, it was his job anyway.

Dave's decision to turn around and land at Saranac Lake Airport is unanimously seconded by me. After explaining to our passengers and Boston Center our intentions, I cancel our flight plan, and graciously accept the radar vectoring to the airport. After changing transponder and radio frequencies I reinform our passengers about the location of the emergency window and check their seat belts. I contact Saranac Lake on the unicom frequency and inform them of our situation; in their response I am given the pertinent information regarding runway and wind conditions. Turning final, the airspeed is a comfortable 130 mph. The gear is extended, and partial flap incorporated, and Dave expertly places the Twin Commanche on the runway. It is now after dark as we taxi toward the light on the nearest hangar.

As we deplane, a tall figure of a man approaches. He is one of the local aircraft mechanics who had overheard our radio transmissions over the Unicom and out of curiosity decides to stay a little longer. He very politely introduces himself and offers to investigate the source of our problem.

Looking at the feathered propeller, then kneeling down he shines his flashlight at the underside of the engine nacelle and wing. Both are covered with oil. Removal of the cowling reveals an oil soaked engine and firewall. Dave and the mechanic engage in conversation.

Two days prior, the airplane received a 100-hour inspection at the Piper Facility in Skaneateles, New York. An oil line for the right engine had been improperly torqued, and from the vibration had dislodged itself. All the oil from the right engine and propeller were released into the engine compartment and eventually overboard.

Much to our pleasant surprise, the mechanic quickly

reinstalls the line, replaces the engine oil, washes down the engine and proceeds with a run up. He then replaces the cowling and deems the airplane airworthy. I file a new flight plan for Albany, a mere 100 nautical miles away; yet still a long flight for four pairs of eyes to watch an oil pressure gauge without blinking.

Our arrival at Albany finds better weather than forecast, after delivering our passengers we fly back to Poestenkill. Midnight finds the two of us in a diner with our steaks. By this time we are so tired it is an effort to chew. I finally break the silence, "Why then?"

"What do you mean?" Dave answers while still chewing his steak.

"Why Saranac Lake? We had found the only whole in the clouds on our entire flight, why did that oil line choose that time to uncouple? Why not Pittsburgh or Flint?" To that question we both knew there was no answer. Right now my only wish is for a soft, warm bed.

Flights to Bradley Field require an aircraft with a larger cargo carrying capability, making the early model Aztec in our fleet quite suitable. Although not as streamlined as the newer Aztecs, the removal of the rear seats for the extra cubic feet of space and two 250 hp engines, it does the job well.

It also serves as our multi-engine training airplane. After a few more flights to Bradley with Dave, I spend several hours flying with Dave in preparation for my flight check. Before I am through, I will draw each system on a blank sheet of paper from memory, with a full explanation of its operation; including the electrical, hydraulic and fuel systems.

One item stands out above all in my mind, understanding the classic twin-engine accident sequence and demonstrating its prevention. On one engine, the aircraft is flown continually slower until full rudder is required to maintain heading (25). If airspeed deterioration is allowed to continue into a stall condition, the aircraft can roll over and enter a spin or spiral. Without altitude, the ground will be contacted before recovery can be accomplished.

Consequently, the pilot is required to demonstrate stall recognition and recovery while operating on one engine. A reduction of power on the good engine and lowering the nose will prevent this sequence from starting. This, however, is inconsistent with a stall recovery in a single engine airplane where full power is required for recovery. Thus the transitional training to multi-engine aircraft is careful, deliberate and can prove to be interesting. Once mastered in the air, the next step is single engine operations during the take-off and landing configurations.

Dave is not one for simulation; instead of simulating an engine failure via throttle reduction, he turns off the fuel flow to the left engine, rendering it inoperative shortly after take off. Once the dead engine is identified, it is imperative to feather the propeller for drag reduction, thus allowing continued flight on one engine.

Departing to the north near rooftop level is definitely an incentive to perform my tasks properly. The only pump providing hydraulic pressure for the flaps and landing gear is mounted on the left engine. Manual operation of a hand pump is now required to operate both the gear and flaps.

After take-off, I manually retract the gear, fly the pattern and extend both gear and flaps manually at specific locations to perform a single engine landing. After established on a final approach, the command for a single engine go-around is issued. This means retracting gear and flaps manually and returning for another landing. The telescoping handle for this pump is located at the bottom of the engine control quadrant; according to the manual, 37 to 42 pumps are required to recycle the gear, while only 14 to 17 are required for the flaps. This is both a physical and mental exercise; flying the airplane while counting the numbers.

Several days later, I walk into a familiar office at Glens Falls where I have an appointment with Guy, "I see you have yourself an airplane with an extra propeller?" I smile as we shake hands.

A lot has changed since the day a 20 year old stood here nervously awaiting his Commercial Pilot Check Ride. Since then I have graduated many students whom Guy has flown with, including Private, Commercial and Instrument Pilots. Our meeting today is very casual, and pleased with Dave's recommendation, the oral and flight tests are strictly academic.

After the check ride, Guy notices the Twin Comanche time in my logbook; which promotes quite the discussion concerning this airplane. During one of Guy's flight tests in a Twin Comanche, the applicant mismanaged flight at slow speed on one engine and entered a spin quite abruptly. Fortunately there was enough altitude for

Guy to recover. It was not long before everyone in the business heard this story. The absence of his generous smile is noticeable as he remarks, "I just thought I would let you know that with this additional rating you are legal to instruct in twin engine aircraft."

I am not so sure I want to hear that.

In the following months, I fly several trips in the Twin Comanche, and the Aztec. A few months later, I am instructing multi-engine students in the Aztec. With most of the students, there are the usual transitional problems; however, up to this point the worst scenario occurred when a student feathered the left engine in his response to my shutting off the fuel to the right engine. With four thousand feet underneath us at the time, the recovery was academic.

A pleasant afternoon finds me over the Tomahannock Reservoir instructing in the Aztec. The preflight instruction on the ground with Mark in preparation for today's session includes the explanation and introduction to single engine stall recoveries. With 800 hours in single engine aircraft, Mark is not exactly a stranger to flying. Once at altitude, I demonstrate the first stall with emphasis on recovery technique and then proceed to turn the controls over to Mark.

After attaining the critical airspeed, before I can stop him, he confidently and abruptly applies full power to the operating engine. The aircraft rolls rapidly to an almost inverted position and continues toward the ground rotating toward the inoperative engine. Apparently the resulting maneuver has shaken him as I yell, "I got it! I got it!" while trying to unfreeze his arm on the throttle. It is amazing how much strength people have under these circumstances.

Finally, with a good jab under his forearm I free his grip on the throttle. Even though my belt is holding me in my seat, I am literally standing on the rudder pedals in an effort to help stop the rotation. Finally, with judicious use of the rudders and throttles, I am able to regain control of the aircraft, and most of my composure.

Mark looks as though he has seen a ghost, and in some way probably has. My displeasure is registered in the tone of my voice, "A diplomat you're not!"

My story follows the one out of Glens Falls.

Flights in the Twin Comanche continue, including frequent trips to Saranac Lake, where on one afternoon Dave is confronted with a rare situation.

The propeller governor on the right engine fails. Thus the propeller control and throttle have become useless, as the runaway propeller is turning beyond its designed maximum RPM.

Instead of making an emergency landing at Saranac Lake, Dave makes the decision to fly the airplane to Skaneateles; a decision we all find hard to understand from a professional pilot's position, particularly when there is a passenger on board.

Reports from Skaneateles reveal that the inner parts of the engine were reduced to chunks of metal. The maintenance department expressed great concern that the airplane had been flown under these conditions considering the strong possibility of fire and even the chance for the loss of the propeller, which could have caused severe damage to the airplane. As a result of this incident, everything from the firewall forward has to be replaced.

During the days that follow, Dave makes lighthearted comments on the loud whining sound the propeller makes even with the extra sound-proofing in the airplane. Even when confronted with the report from Skaneateles on the condition of the engine and how close he had come to fire or structural failure; with a puff of his cheeks as he exhales, while looking toward the floor with his fisheye look he explain, "Well, we made it, and besides, it would have taken too much time getting all the parts to Saranac Lake for repairs".

This is thought to be a poor excuse for a poor excuse; it seems to be part of his personality to revel whenever he pushes the limits without having to pay the consequences.

There is a certain amount of risk involved in our profession; the amount of which is calculable and acceptable considering the rewards. However, there are limitations; understanding our limitations as pilots and the limitations of the equipment we fly is the name of the game. Emergency procedures are written and practiced for a reason - to insure longevity. To deliberately step beyond this boundary is to tug on the Devil's Cape.

Two months after the airplane is returned to service, another problem surfaces. The vents for the wing tip tanks are prone to holding any condensation buildup, something that is not readily seen on a normal preflight. As a result, at altitude, the vents have a tendency to freeze.

On a trip to Watertown, Dave loses the right engine shortly after reaching altitude. I have the same experience on a trip to Baltimore. At this point Dave holds the record for the most engine failures from take off to 10,000 feet; I am second with only one. On both occasions, the engine loss was due to an obstructed fuel vent, thus a service bulletin issued on the airplane included a new procedure for checking the fuel vents (26).

A few months later, the airplane is replaced, bringing smiles to a few faces.

Chapter Nine

Milwaukee or Bust

The lights on the eastern shore of Lake Michigan slide smoothly beneath the wings of the Aztec as I head home. Checking my time crossing the Muskegon VORTAC, my first checkpoint departing Milwaukee, I discover that I am already three minutes ahead of schedule and back into the Eastern Time zone. The remainder of the flight will be as planned; direct to Flint, direct Sarnia Canada, Victor 208 Buffalo, Victor 14 Albany, and direct Poestenkill, without a fuel stop. This is one of three weekly roundtrip night flights to Milwaukee, where I have just delivered the advertising plates to the publisher. I return the flight plan (27) to the pouch next to my seat and comply with a frequency change from center. I am enjoying the night as I check the time; 1:55 am EST, and start to reflect on past flights. The Aztec is new, with an increased gross weight to 5,200 pounds, comfortable seating and very well equipped.

There is much learned on these flights, not the least which is to make sure the waitress at the coffee shop in Milwaukee does not fill my thermos to the top, because in the less dense air at 9,000 feet, the coffee expands and spills when opened. I know the night lineman who drives us over to the coffee shop for an early breakfast and updates us on the latest news surrounding Billy Mitchell Airport. Lighting my pipe at altitude, the oxygen does not readily support combustion and requires too many matches; henceforth smoking is confined to the ground. I reflect on the array of students and pilots more than willing to ride right seat with me for the experience and a chance to witness the occasional grand display of northern lights over Lake Michigan.

Another new friend I have made is known to me simply as Cleveland Center. I, on the other hand, am known as Aztec 6751 Yankee. One evening, our conversation reveals that he is studying for his Private Pilot Written and that I am an instructor. While traversing his airspace, the lack of traffic allows me to tutor him on his assignments. This airborne ground school lasts for the entire winter.

All the pilots chosen to fly to Milwaukee are required to fly route familiarization flights with Dave Carling. During some of these flights, keeping a close watch on the weather is as interesting as flying the airplane. On one such flight, a stationary front lingered for a few days in the Milwaukee and Chicago areas resulting in delays and cancellations. Approaching Flint, Michigan, we are informed that Milwaukee is below limits and forecasted to remain so for the next eight hours. Thus we choose Chicago as our alternate, requiring a fuel stop at Flint, Michigan, before proceeding to our new destination.

Approaching Chicago, the weather is 200 overcast 1/8-mile visibility. The ILS approach requires 200-1/2; consequently we are assigned a holding pattern at 2,000 feet. While flying the assigned holding pattern, it is interesting to note the contrast between the star-studded skies and the blanket of fog covering the airport. Portions of the city are quite visible from our location which leads to a conversation punctuated with laughter as to who decides to put the airport here instead of over there.

Periodically, I check for any increase in the surface winds, hoping for a wind of seven knots or greater; this is usually enough to move the fog and increase visibility. After about 45 minutes, this becomes a reality, and we are cleared for the approach.

As the airplane enters the fog, each wing tip has a corresponding colored ring around each navigation light, while the reflection of the landing light off the small water particles in the fog make it seem much denser. The smooth air makes capturing and flying the localizer and glide slope academic. As I report the outer marker, we are cleared to land; within seconds, we are informed that the visibility is rapidly diminishing.

I call out our altitude every 100 feet until we reach decision height at the middle marker; here I have contact with the high intensity approach lights sequentially flashing in the direction of a runway I cannot see. Once over the approach lights, the relatively dim runway lights welcome us as we touch down on one foggy Chicago Runway.

The hardest part of the approach is to find the taxiways to and from the runway as the visibility drops to 1/8 mile shortly after landing.

We make arrangements for the advertising plates to be driven to Milwaukee. After refueling, we prepare for our departure; this is accomplished with about 1/8 mile visibility.

Our cargo, weighing approximately five pounds, is delivered to us each evening between 9 pm and midnight.

E. A. Chevrette, Jr.

Shortly after takeoff from Poestenkill, Albany approach control responds with an immediate clearance to our destination.

This particular evening, there is a well-defined warm front along our flight; in the winter this type of front produces precipitation in the form of freezing rain. After twenty minutes of flight in the leading edge of the front, we acquire a fair amount of structural ice accumulation. Once established in the warm air, the temperature rises to a plus one-Celsius. The precipitation turns to rain with conditions remaining this way until we reach Muskegon and we are clear of the precipitation for the remainder of the flight.

The son of a controller at the Albany Airport is returning home from Milwaukee for spring break, so arrangements have been made for him to ride with us on our return trip. After locating our passenger, we have breakfast and return to the pilot lounge.

On a previous trip, I had noticed a large aquarium in the pilot lounge containing some large goldfish. One of them was not as active as the rest and, according to the lineman, this one was not long for the world. We started kidding each other about remedies for goldfish, and laughed at our cluelessness concerning the subject. In our grand wisdom we thought a good whiskey, poured into the tank, would either kill or cure the fish.

Walking over to the tank, I find all the fish doing well. The lineman looks at me with a big grin, "We did it!" he says.

"Did what?" I ask.

"We put about a half a pint of Scotch in the tank last

148

week, and they've been swimming like crazy ever since!"

We both laugh out loud. At this point, Dave comes into the room and when he realizes the situation, he joins in the laughter, and exclaims, "Those fish have expensive taste!"

Leaving Milwaukee, Dave takes the left seat and, leveling at 9,000 feet we settle down. For the next three hours all we see is rain. I monitor the forecasts along our route, digesting each with a grain of salt as we prepare to combat the other enemy of these flights; fatigue.

I awake to the Center calling our number. Suddenly, I am horror-stricken; I am the only one awake in the airplane. I notice we are still relatively on course as I reach over and adjust the heading control on the autopilot. It must be time to change center frequency, as our controller is making the necessary communications. I have no idea how long he has been calling our number; answering as nonchalantly as possible I hope he will not question any tardiness in my reply. Much to my relief, there is just a confirmation of my transmission.

Checking our time, position and fuel, I realize it is Thursday morning. Including my daytime duties, I have not seen a bed since Tuesday night. I turn on the overhead vent full blast and reach down to the bottom center of the throttle console to reduce the cabin heat. We have been given a reprieve from disaster.

I slap my face a few times, half to wake up, half as punishment for this careless act. I turn and straight-arm Dave's right shoulder and yell, "Wake up!" He awakes and asks our position. I find his casualness so maddening, I want to hit him; this alone is enough to keep my adrenaline going for the rest of the flight.

Upon our arrival, the weather has improved, making an initial approach at Albany unnecessary. Flying back into the colder air we are confronted by another situation; rain accumulating in the elevator trim tab has frozen, rendering the trim control unusable. With both of us on the controls, we are able to pull the control wheel far enough aft to accomplish an uneventful landing.

No flight, however, is as memorable as that of January 9. I check the weather late in the afternoon. There is a possibility of a mild winter storm over the lakes at our departure time, possibly producing some sleet, but it is thought to be of little consequence for our flight, considering the time of day we will encounter it, the top of the clouds should be low enough to permit a flight on top.

I walk into the hangar to find Dave applying ICEX (28) on the pneumatic deicing boots, and the electric boots on the props. Looking at the can I remark, "Looks like I might learn something tonight."

Dave replies; "We both might learn something tonight."

With that, I prepare for our departure.

Heading westbound, with the lights of the tri-city area behind us, Dave reports us level at 8,000 feet. I set the airplane up for best cruise, install my armrest and prepare to enjoy the flight. Both engines are synchronized at 2,400 RPM; with the correction for altitude and temperature, the airspeed indicator reads a true 203 MPH. I look out the windshield at a beautiful star-studded winter night and think it a crime, punishable by death, to intrude such an evening with a winter storm.

Approaching Syracuse, we enter the clouds and encounter sleet. I check the outside temperature reading; minus two degrees Celsius. The sound at first is quite noticeable as the sleet hits the clean windshield. Dave turns on the pitot heat and activates the electric props. One piece of ice protection not available at the time, for this airplane is a heated windshield, an item worth our envy before the night is through.

Frequent turbulence now accompanies the precipitation. As if we need something to occupy our hands, Dave turns on the landing light. I watch in an almost hypnotic trance as the speed of the airplane is reflected on the constant waves of heavy precipitation being pumped through the atmosphere.

I lean forward, placing my arms on top of the instrument panel, as if in gesture for a closer look. There are small glowing wormlike displays of static electricity moving across the windshield, congregating in the corners before being discharged into the atmosphere. As I turn in my seat to observe the left propeller for any similar displays, I inadvertently touch the center post of the windshield and feel a very slight jolt, as if I am being slapped on the hand for reaching for the forbidden cookie jar.

Within minutes, the windshield is opaque with ice, deadening the sound of the sleet. I shine my light on the left de-icing boot, as the ice accumulation that resembles pie crust, now cracks and disappears in small chunks as Dave activates the system for the first time tonight.

The ice has made its introduction; careful monitoring is necessary.

What sounds like marbles being thrown against the sides of the fuselage near the nose is the ice being shed by the propellers. This sound will continue intermittently throughout the remainder of the flight.

Passing Buffalo, we are still in the clouds; our departure forecast puts us out of the storm at this point. Dave checks with the center, which then reports both Syracuse and Buffalo are below limits; the storm has increased in strength and now stretches to the eastern shore of Lake Michigan. There are no available reports for cloud tops or icing ahead of us.

I reach for our flight plan and turn on the overhead cabin light; this seems more of an intrusion than a necessary act. The pre- printed flight plan for this route is like a scorecard - head winds vs. airspeed and time in the air. Positive points put us ahead of schedule, with more fuel reserve, however we are running negative points; Dave half nods in acknowledgement as we continue.

The rate of ice accumulation is very concerning. Dave has been activating the boots at very close intervals. The actual boots are relatively clean; however, a ridge of ice has formed around the perimeter of each, taking more of a toll on the aerodynamics of this airplane. Each wing tip light has a Plexiglass reflector for monitoring at night; these are now ice-covered.

The airspeed indicator reflects the added drag and weight; 185 MPH. The windshield resembles the inside of a cocoon. Neither one of us is saying anything about the leading edge of the wing between each engine nacelle and the fuselage. This part of the airplane is completely unprotected from any ice accumulation.

We are approaching Sarnia, Canada. On clear nights, or even on top of a cloud layer, the bright glow of the steel mill is easy to spot, usually leading to a conversation about the same; tonight there is little conversation. Turning on the overhead light, I watch the stabilizer trim control handle on the ceiling move slightly while changing the trim setting indicator accordingly. Through the autopilot, it automatically retrims the airplane to compensate for changes in air speed, which has been constantly diminishing. It does this without ever knowing the reason why.

Force of habit has me reaching behind Dave's seat for a look at our flight plan, as though a piece of paper would have an answer to all this. The Cleveland Center calls with good news: Flint is now open. With that Dave announces; "Forget the flight plan, we're going into Flint, change seats now!"

I unfasten my seatbelt and start to move the left seat aft. I glance at the airspeed indicator which rivets my attention; the needle has passed 153 MPH and is continuing its search for lower numbers. I can feel a sense of urgency as we switch seats.

Once accomplished, Dave asks me to hand him a glove and the scraper that he placed behind the left seat. I comply. He places the glove on his left hand, opens the storm window located on the pilot's side and attempts to reach forward to scrape the ice from the windshield. I watch this maneuver with interest and disbelief; I am particularly attentive when he winces as the wind forces his arm away from the windshield and back behind his head. He then brings his hand inside and reattempts to repeat his performance without the scraper.

"Dave!" I actually chuckle, "That is not going to work, you're going to break your arm!"

Nodding in agreement, he closes the window. I see the look on his face. As experienced as he is, something is wrong. A chill grips my whole body, fear is present and I can feel it. It has been said that any man who does not admit to fear, at least to himself, is either a fool or a liar. Tonight I am neither. There is much work to do and not much time to do it; I must escape its filthy presence.

I pull out the approach plate for Flint Michigan, at the same time informing the center of our intentions. He immediately responds with a clearance to 4,000 feet, which is where this machine is headed anyway. I glance at the meter that monitors the electric propeller anti-icing. It is confirming 30-second intervals of electricity to each propeller blade element...

"Aztec 6751 Yankee, pilot reports 400 overcast 1 mile sleet, reported by a Cessna 402 twenty minutes ago." The controller's voice is prompt and quick, and probably more understanding of our predicament than I give him credit for. Sometimes it is reassuring to know someone else is out there with you, as it is normal for a pilot to ask for flight conditions experienced by another aircraft ahead of him.

"Any icing reports?"

As if I did not know. "Nothing reported." The next

transmission clears us for an ILS approach to runway nine.

As we pass The Flint VORTAC, approach control changes us to the tower frequency. I inform Dave that I have the #1 navigational radio set up for the ILS, #2 set up for the Vortac as per the published missed approach procedure. This we both know is not going to happen.

We are not in a radar environment, thus we are required to fly a procedure turn. Flying the ILS outbound from the outer marker for one minute, we then execute the procedure turn. This maneuver, diagrammed on the approach chart I am holding, shows a forty-five-degree turn to the right. After 60 seconds, a 180-degree left turn. This is the procedure turn inbound; from here we will intercept the localizer with a forty-five degree left turn toward the runway. The entire procedure must be flown at or above a published minimum altitude, normally taking about five-minutes. Once inbound on the localizer, glide slope interception is accomplished at the outer marker; from here the final approach is flown to the runway.

The marker beacon confirms our passage of the middle marker, while the outer marker passage is confirmed by the ADF needle and the marker beacon, "Tower, 51 Yankee outer- marker outbound."

"51 Yankee, report procedure turn inbound."

I acknowledge. All engine gauges read normal; the two Lycoming engines have performed flawlessly throughout the flight, while the fuel gauges reflect the additional fuel used for the conditions.

Dave starts his turn outbound as I call out our

minimum altitude. We both look at the altimeter and rate of climb indicator. Both instruments confirm a bone chilling fact; due to the structural ice, we are no longer able to hold altitude.

Dave's response is immediate, "Tell'em we're inbound." Our only chance is to actually fly against all normal procedures: an immediate right turn toward the outer marker while at the same time trying to keep the bank to a minimum to avoid much more altitude loss, or worse, stalling.

I announce to the tower. "51 Yankee inbound."

"51 Yankee, are you reporting procedure turn inbound?" I must have confused him momentarily, for I had just reported the outer marker outbound. He probably did not expect to hear from me for five minutes, five minutes we do not have.

I confirm his transmission. "Ok 51 Yankee, weather 400 and 1, cleared to land. Report the outer marker."

I acknowledge I will comply with his request.

Trying to capture the localizer and the glide slope at the outer marker all at once in good weather is a feat of near magical proportions, but on a night such as this... "Give me full power!" Dave has both hands on the wheel and is desperately trying to keep us aloft and minimize our rate of descent. I hold my breath as both engines snarl when the prop controls are placed in low pitch, followed by full throttles; so far we are still in the air.

The ADF needle and the marker beacon receiver confirm our crossing the outer marker. We are slightly below the minimum crossing altitude, and just below the glide slope. I slide my seat back one notch, refasten my seatbelt and look out the rear corner of the wrap-around windshield for any signs of the ground. Dave reaches over and reluctantly places the gear handle into the down position. I watch intently, half expecting any additional drag on this machine to be its demise. His next action is the deployment of flaps.

"Still in the clouds, still in the clouds..." I repeat.

I pick up the reflection of the approach lights as the airplane nears the base of the clouds. "Approach lights coming up!" I hope there is enough lift in these wings to keep from hitting the elevated steel supports the approach lights are mounted on. If not, this will be the end of the road in more ways than one.

"Ground contact!" This looks awfully close for 400 feet. Just a few more seconds, that is all we need, a few more seconds. At that point the marker beacon verifies our position, only ½ mile to go.

"Middle marker!" Just a little bit more, if we can just get to the end of the runway...

"Threshold underneath us!" This in itself is a great relief; pavement has a tendency to be more user friendly than suspended approach lights, rocks or trees. Power has not been fully reduced before the wheels contact the runway with a definite bump. There is no more life left in these wings.

I have heard, jokingly, that any landing you can walk away from is a good one; this one will go down in my personal hall of fame.

On the roll out, all we can see is either side of the

runway out of our respective windows. I open the door to kneel on the wing walk because from there I can direct us to the ramp. The sleet stings my face. Using the opened door as a shield, I navigate from behind the Plexiglass side window. This is the only forward visibility we have.

Once positioned on the ramp, I approach the end of the wing walk and look down at the step, which is totally unrecognizable due to the accumulation of ice. Sitting on the wing walk I kick the step free of ice to make it useable. The lineman greets me at the right wing tip with a whistle. "This one is worse than that Cessna parked over there." I glance at the Cessna 402, finding that it has accumulated half as much ice as ours.

The wing tip light located at the arc of the wing tip is completely covered. From there I continue to the leading edge of the wing for the rest of the scenario. The deicing boot itself is fairly clean; I estimate the ridge of ice that has formed around the entire boot, in some areas approaches almost an inch. I start to pound at the well-hardened ice with my gloved hands and gradually work my way to the right engine.

The speed fairing between the leading edge and the nacelle, which is not exposed to the full impact of ice, has over two inches. The engine cowling has a grizzly look about it, as does the propeller spinner. I continue pounding on the ice ridge around the boots and work my way toward the engine cowling.

Visual inspection of the propeller is a testament to electric props; the blades are clean. The air intake at the bottom of the nacelle is almost closed off with ice. As I approach the section of wing between the fuselage and engine nacelle, I realize Dave is standing behind me with a flashlight. This is a good indication as to how much ice we have actually accumulated.

In the light, a sickening sight is revealed: we estimate at least five inches of ice has accumulated on the leading edge of the wing. The light is then directed toward the nose. With this, we discover that the entire nose, almost unrecognizable, is covered from where the landing light is supposed to be, back to and over the windshield. I look at Dave, whose facial expression is of total disbelief and exclaim, "Jesus." It is at this point we realize that this flight is not half over yet. A condition of our contract for these flights is a guaranteed delivery.

At the tail section, I find myself hanging onto a flimsy aluminum stepladder, flailing my arms against the ice that has completely covered the rotating beacon on top of the vertical fin. I imagine the morning headlines, "Aztec pilot killed falling off aluminum stepladder." Dave laughs when I tell him. It takes over an hour to de-ice the airplane. When finished, I go inside to pay for the fuel while Dave files our flight plan.

Jokingly, the lineman says, "Lovely weather for ducks."

My reply; "No self-respecting duck would be out in weather like this!"

Departing the pilot lounge, I notice two tired-looking pilots standing at the window. For tonight, at least, this is their home. When asked of our destination, I reply. The senior of the two wishes us luck.

As I approach the airplane, Dave has the left engine running. The lineman has already cleaned off what sleet has accumulated during refueling.

I climb inside and contact ground control, "Ground, Aztec 6751 Yankee taxiing, instruments to..." I pause, looking to Dave as he starts the right engine. I continue my message into the microphone "....Milwaukee", *(releasing the mic button),* or bust."

By the time we reach the active runway, we are cleared to Milwaukee at 8,000 feet and cleared for take off. The airplane seems to leap off the ground as if in a sigh of relief to be rid of the ice.

Within a few minutes of our departure, I am exercising the boots again and wondering what the rest of the night might bring. When in a cloud, a halo forms around the wing tip lights, a place where the largest accumulation of ice can also be found. I call the Center to request a cruise clearance between 4,000 to 8,000 feet, which will allow us to change altitude without requesting a separate clearance. By changing altitude frequently, we can fly between layers of clouds minimizing the accumulation of ice. On one particular change to 8,000 feet, I glance up at a star-studded sky. "We're on top!"

Our relief is expressed in our chattering, like a couple of schoolboys who have just won the championship for their hometown team. Toward the end of the conversation, I look down at two control handles located on the bottom of the throttle pedestal where one finds the alternate source of induction air for the engines in the event the air intakes become clogged with ice. They were never used.

The rest of the flight to Milwaukee is without conversation except for air traffic control.

Few words pass between Dave and me during an early morning breakfast of pancakes and sausage. We finish our coffee and return to the airplane. A few minutes later we are eastbound at 9,000 feet sporting a good tail wind, which will make this leg a lot shorter. Normally, the entire trip takes 7 ½ to 8 hours. The first half of this flight had taken slightly over five hours.

Approximately 100 miles west of Albany, my frequent requests for higher altitudes to stay on top find us at 11,000 feet. All we are doing is prolonging the inevitable, although the main part of this storm is to the east of our destination, making flight under these conditions considerably less difficult. What remains of the storm is still a factor.

Boston Center hands us over to Albany Approach with a clearance for a descent. Within moments, the windshield is opaque with ice and rendered useless, as once again we encounter icing conditions. We are to expect a clearance for the ILS to Albany which will lead us to weather conditions good enough for a visual flight to home base.

Breaking out of the clouds on the approach to Albany, we depart for home while discussing the strategy for landing. A 2,800-foot runway whose surface is not as good as Flint, nor does it possess an ILS or approach lights, in combination with our fatigue should prove this landing to be quite interesting. Dave has made many landings to the north occupying the left seat. I, as an instructor, the same, but while occupying the right seat of our respective airplanes. This prompts us to exchange seats one more time.

We approach Poestenkill and decide that a landing to the north will be the easier approach with the fewest obstacles. We assess our icing condition and find less than half the accumulation as compared to Flint. With the rising sun, daylight is now our best friend.

As we make our final approach, we discover this landing to be not as easily done as said, regardless of our preplanned strategy. Even with our ice accumulation, we actually manage a go around. On downwind, Dave tries again to reach out and scrape some ice off the windshield, but again, to no avail. A wide left turn onto final approach is executed to better align with the runway.

We do not have the luxury of 100-foot wide runways with snow banks pushed back another few feet. Our very own snow banks are just a few feet wider than each wing tip. We have agreed that once on the ground, we will watch for the snow banks on either side of the runway. Should the right side of the runway get too close, I will apply left rudder. Dave would do the opposite from the other side. The airplane cannot be flown too slowly, we still have ice to contend with. On the other hand, it cannot be flown too fast either, as we will use up runway space we do not have.

As we fly the final approach, we call out to each other the familiar landmarks on either side of the airplane. Approaching the runway threshold, I move my seat forward and hold onto the brace bar just inside the windshield. This way I can plant my feet on the rudder pedals on my side of the airplane.

"Road coming up on the south side of the runway... got it..." Dave acknowledges.

"Power wires, the runway is real close now!"

Crossing the threshold, we simultaneously call for power off. With a definite bump, we contact the runway. We are both on the rudder pedals and brakes simultaneously, keeping the airplane straight while trying to stop...

"Dave, right side coming up. Got it?"

"Yeah... hang on. Left side coming your way..."

"Got it, coming your way again."

Each time I depress a brake pedal I can feel one of the main wheels start to skid. Dave is holding the control wheel full back, power at idle... I can feel the machine slowing, and finally we bring the airplane to a halt.

"Whew!"

"Good morning Poestenkill."

As the flaps are retracted and power added to the right engine to aid our 180-degree turn on the runway, the right wing is over the snow bank, just before the trees, which is the absolute end of the runway. I am actually glad the windshield is covered with ice.

We park the airplane in one of the unheated hangars. As we leave, Dave makes mention of the fact that now everyone can look at the machine to see what ice looks like. At that point, I wonder how much of this is for ego... then again, I am too tired to care.

Arriving home, I walk into a quiet kitchen, for which

I am very grateful. I place my coat and still dampened gloves on the table. Rummaging through the cabinets for a pen, I come across an open bottle of Canadian Club. For a moment, I cannot decide if this flight requires a drink, or deserves one; either way, I reach for a glass.

Opening my logbook, I ponder some of the events of this flight: the events leading up to Flint, Michigan; the return trip home. With all the experience Dave has, I do not think even he has ever flown an airplane so laden with ice. As for myself, I almost stayed home to stave off this cold. I am now too tired to analyze all that transpired on this flight. In the remarks column of my logbook I simply make a note; turbulence and ice. I look at my still damp gloves and finish my drink, and wonder if the Canadian Club will have the same effect on me as the scotch did for the fish.

After the flights to Milwaukee end, the controller from Cleveland Center whom I had tutored from the left seat of the Aztec, tracks me through the flight plans and the Albany Air Traffic Controllers. I receive a thank you note. He passed his written exam.

A few years after, Guy Scram out of Glens Falls had a similar situation with icing in his Aztec. He is fortunate enough to walk away from the wreckage with only minor injuries.

About the same time, Dave oversteps the boundaries of his luck. Trying to sneak into Poestenkill on a foggy night, he misjudges and flies into the hill behind the airport. This cost him his life.

Although saddened by the misfortune of my colleagues, the value of what was learned is immeasurable.

Chapter Ten

All In a Day's Work

Don Mulligan and Lou Slatterly have been friends for several years, both men well known in the aviation community, the latter for his past seaplane operations at Round Lake, New York. The airport, located on the east side of the lake, and the seaplane base have both been inactive for several years. After several meetings, both men decide to reopen operations at Round Lake.

It is a very cold wintry day when I become aware of what is in the works. Since I am not exactly a seaplane expert, I jokingly, yet politely, question the great minds that plan the reopening of a seaplane operation on a frozen lake supporting who knows how much snow. Of course, there is the airport, which has not seen a snow plow all winter. Locating the northwest, southeast runway with adjoining taxiway and tie-down ropes will be a near miracle in itself. After a good laugh, Don looks at me..."It should prove interesting!" It does.

My first touchdown at our new location is on the frozen snow that covers the lake. This make-shift runway will serve our purposes until we uncover the airport's runway.

As the sun starts to set, tall, thin Ted, who bares a resemblance to Ichabod Crane, joins Don and myself for a cigarette and some conversation. Here are three grown men, huddled around three airplanes in the middle of a frozen lake watching the shore line for signs of life. Ted's voice is of deep tone as he slowly speaks, "We must look like a bunch of boot-leggers sneaking in and out of the frozen lake when no one is looking." Pulling his collar up and his hat down over his eyes, "Maybe we should call this the Round Lake Caper." With that, we all break out in such laughter we could hardly speak.

That evening, when all is done, two airplanes are left on the lake, tied down to cement blocks we carried out earlier. The third airplane takes the three of us back to Albany Airport.

The next morning, I drive down the access road to the airport, and park next to an old "T" hanger with attached office. Across the parking lot is a long narrow block building; this is the main hangar. Walking past the hangar, I look to the south at what will soon be our main taxiway, where I see a familiar airplane - one that had been parked on the lake the night before. I then recognize the figure walking around the airplane in the unplowed snow; it is Mulligan.

As I arrive at the Cessna 150, I notice Don has shoveled down to the ground in front of the nose gear. The nose wheel itself is sitting on snow six inches higher than the ground with the top of the snow equally as deep. There are also tell- tale wheel tracks in the unplowed snow covering the runway. These tracks start from nowhere, and stay on top of the crust of snow until just a few feet from where the airplane is presently parked; here they have sunk deeper into the snow. Snow this deep can easily flip an airplane, a shear wonder I thought, had I not known the man who made the tracks. My only regret is not having witnessed the event personally. Brushing some of the snow away from the airplane, he greets me with a smile and an L&M cigarette in his mouth, "Good morning, thought we might have a cup of coffee to start the day." I return the salutation with a smile while slightly shaking my head.

We return to the hangar building for our coffee, where I am introduced to Lou. Slightly bow-legged and in his sixties, he speaks in deliberate sentences. His speech seems labored, which results in a high pitch, almost whining sound. Very congenial and quite observant, he invited me on a tour of the hangar building.

Once inside the hangar that Lou had designed and built, a light switch I believe to be of early electric vintage activates the overhead lights. The floor, supplied by Mother Nature, is pure dirt. There are handmade hangar doors whose external shape are curved to fit snugly against the overhead beams when opened, and door jams when closed. Concrete blocks are actually suspended on either side of each door in handmade rope harnesses for counterbalance. I am somewhat surprised to see the relative ease of their operation just by pulling on a rope attached to an overhead pulley. Once open, the counterbalances are located just high enough off the floor as not to be a hindrance. The noise generated by our presence and the opening of the doors, does not seem to disturb the resident birds, both natural and man-made.

I emerge from the hangar to look at the Tetrahedron (29). It seems ideally located south of the main runway where it can be reached by the wind to indicate landing direction without interference form nearby trees. This also has been hand built; the torn fabric covering it is in need of repair. Standing in front of the hangar, I brake through the crust of snow spilling my coffee. After finding better footing, I finish what is left and ask about the condition of the Tetrahedron and its accuracy.

"Works well. I'm going to replace the fabric with aluminum and brightly colored paint for easy recognition."

Meanwhile, we need a temporary runway until the airport is open. We make one; from the intersection of the taxiway and main runway, we plow a strip to the southeast, somewhat less than 500 feet long and 40 feet wide, with 2-foot snow banks around the perimeter.

Take-offs are accomplished to the southeast; twenty degrees of flap and literally pulling the airplane off the ground in a semi-stall condition until sufficient speed is attained for a climb. This is accomplished regardless of the wind conditions. Landings and approaches are flown in the opposite direction, with full flaps and enough power once reduced to result in a full stall landing right at the end of the runway. We clear an area at the northwest end of our runway for parking the airplanes, which only adds to the necessity to stop in time.

It is a typical late winter afternoon following the passage of a cold front; airplanes are tugging at their tie down ropes while being abused by high winds with peak gusts. Accompanying snow squalls reduce visibility to just a few feet.

Inside the small office, a conversation is in progress between Don and me concerning the addition of a floatplane to the fleet. Lou enters the office and joins us. The discussion concerns the purchase of a Cessna 170 and a set of floats to fit the airplane. Lou adds to the discussion concerning one hangar he will set aside for converting the airplane from wheels to floats. The strategy for the actual conversion is discussed and will be finalized by early spring.

As we lock up the office for the day, Lou turns to me and asks if I have ever flown a Link Trainer. They are simulators, built in Binghamton, New York, and used extensively during the war for pilot training.

The Link is shaped like an airplane with control surfaces actuated from inside the small cockpit to give the student the basic understanding of controlled flight. The unit is mounted on several bellows on top of a pedestal allowing movement around its axis similar to that of an actual airplane. On top of the unit is a canopy that could be closed by the instructor, rendering the unit useful for instrument flight simulation.

Mounted on top of a large desk adjacent to the link is a tracking device which marks the course the trainer has flown on a piece of Plexiglas that covers an aeronautical chart. These machines require considerable floor space, are of considerable weight, consume a generous amount of electricity, and are far from being portable. After discussing the pros and cons of these simulators there comes an invitation.

"I have a few simulators in my basement, would you be interested in having a look?"

My curiosity will not allow me to say anything but yes.

The basement of his house is much larger than most, and like most, housekeeping is not a high priority. After removing some clutter, the first simulator he built is exposed.

Although not resembling the shape of an airplane, it does have an instrument panel; complete with operating controls, switches and radios. Mounted on top of the device is a tracker to mark the progress of each flight. I operate this machine through some basic instrument flight maneuvers strictly for my familiarization; I am suitably impressed with the ease of operation and relatively small amount of floor space required.

Lou removes a drop cloth from what I think to be a piece of small furniture, "Tell me what do you think of this?"

He proceeds to uncover two portable flight simulators, each approximately the size of a portable television set. Each self-standing unit weighs approximately 50 pounds with removable legs for placing on top of a table.

The instrument panel is complete with all the instruments found in an actual airplane, with the face of the simulator angled for easy monitoring of the instruments. Included in this are the navigational instruments for each radio he has built into each simulator.

As I sit in front of one of these portable devices, I cannot help but notice the great detail of each instrument and radio receiver. He does not use actual aircraft instruments or radios due to weight and cost. Each instrument and radio control is hand made to the exact replication and operation of a real instrument panel. All the pieces, including plastic cabinetry, have to be made in molds he himself builds.

Two small electric motors are built into each unit, which in turn operate all this equipment via small pulleys and control wires that he has constructed; all this operates from a standard 110-volt outlet. Although each simulator is stationary, there is still a considerable amount of concentration required when flying one.

The tracking device, of similar size and construction, weighs approximately 30 pounds, and uses a common marking pen placed in a holder to follow the progress of each flight over a plastic-covered chart. The trainer and tracking device can be equipped with a variety of frequencies, all depending on the chart to be used, including any standard instrument approach.

Through an umbilical cord between the trainer and tracking device, it is possible to simulate and track an instrument cross-country flight and approach using any approved enroute chart or approach plate.

I am given the opportunity to engage these machines as part of my instrument instruction program I would be conducting that winter. I find the simulators to be a good instructional aid, and when used accordingly produce good results; it is disheartening that these machines were never marketed beyond this basement.

It is a pleasant spring morning in 1971 as I enter the hangar where The Cessna 170 is supported by heavy-duty ropes from the purposely-designed hangar rafters. The transition from wheels to floats is close to completion with the first flight expected early this afternoon.

The hangar door is opened, and a rather strange-looking device is backed into the hangar and placed under the floats of the airplane. This device, is slightly longer than the floats, and incorporates two fifteen-inch truck wheels mounted on either side of a steel frame. Just inside of the four wheels are two wood platforms that support the floats. With the exception of the steel structure connecting the sides, the space between the wood platforms is open. Outside of each platform are vertical guides made of angle iron with wood bumpers covered with sections of old tires to guide the loading and unloading of the airplane. These vertical guides also support a wooden walkway along either side.

The Cessna is carefully lowered via block and tackle onto the wood platforms. Once untied, a Ford Tractor tows the airplane down to the edge of the lake. With a rope tied to the head of one float, the airplane is then backed down a shale ramp into the lake until it floats. Don, who is standing on the wooden platform, unties the rope, steps onto the float and the airplane is launched.

Standing on the shore, I watch Lou on the tractor, puffing on his pipe between issuing instructions for launching the Cessna. I ask him who the manufacturer of the launch vehicle is.

Without takings his eye off the launching, laughs and replies; "It's all in a days work I guess."

On the way down to the shoreline, Lou and Don are discussing who will be the first to fly the machine now that it was ready for the water. It has been a couple of years since Don has flown the water, and his wish is to have Lou on board for this maiden flight.

Chuck Cross, an instructor and mechanic, joins our company. A balding man, the crow's feet around his squinting eyes reflect his experience, yet does not hide his sense of humor. He always has a knack for lightening things, frequently using Lou as the nucleus, referencing Lou as the Great One and questioning how we could we survive without him, or addressing him as the Great Psychic Medium and Master of float flying. How he could actually do this with a straight face is amazing.

With Don at the controls, the Cessna is now floating on its own. Lou is on the shore next to the launching rig, with hands cupped on either side of his face, giving Don some last minute information, "The water is not too rough, so your first take-off should be relatively easy."

"Lou, don't you want to see how it flies?"

"I suppose so."

"Well hop on board."

As the conversation continues, we all begin to laugh. Chuck motions me to grab a length of rope, which in turn is thrown to Don. Still laughing, Chuck suggests that Lou show us how he can walk on water and save us the extra work. Lou replies," It cannot be done without getting his sandals wet." This only adds to the laughter already in progress.

Of the four of us at the lake that day, three possess a single and multi-engine water rating, which is rare for pilots of this geographic area. Although not water rated, I enjoy the ensuing demonstration put on with the Cessna 170.

The lake itself is approximately one mile across, almost perfectly round in shape and appropriately named. With the exception of the small tributary that joins a similarly shaped and considerably smaller body of water on the northeast side, trees surround most of the lake's perimeter.

Katie, Don's wife, joins Lou and me today for my first official flight on water. The airplane is sitting in shallow water making it very easy to step over onto one of the floats and enter the cabin. Katie occupies the rear seat and I fasten myself into the right seat while Don and Lou cast the airplane off into deeper water.

As the airplane drifts away from the shore, Lou is standing on the left float holding the door open while instructing me, while I slowly maneuver around a couple of small boats, Lou has not changed his position. I glance back at Katie, and judging by the look on her face I determine that she must be thinking the same as I am. With a smile on my face I invite Lou to step inside the airplane. Looking at me Lou laughs, "You've been hanging around Chuck too long."

Lou continues his conversation, "The water is glassy today, with this weight it is best we make some waves to chop up the surface; this will help the floats break the tension of the water." After a few moments of water taxi and some basic instructions on sailing the airplane, Lou climbs inside raises the water rudder and demonstrates our first take-off.

He holds the control wheel in the full aft position while applying full power. As we accelerate, the nose pitches up against the force of the water leaving only the aft part of the floats in the water. As we reach the point where the airplane cannot gain any more speed, the next phase of the take off commences.

Lou pushes forward on the wheel, and starts a rocking motion to get the floats to sit on top of the water. I am impressed at the amount of water these floats are displacing, while at the same time trying to overcome the drag in order to gain speed.

Once the airplane is positioned on the step, we continue to accelerate on top of the water; each wave we hit sends a jolt throughout the entire airplane and down our backbones. Now that the airplane is on top of the water, Lou demonstrates a "step turn", pushing the rudder in the direction of the turn, and opposite aileron to keep the wings level. The shape of the lake provides an endless runway as we accelerate.

Once we have gained as much speed as possible, Lou lifts the right float out of the water, gains a little more speed on the left float until we are airborne at tree-top level. We continue at this altitude until the wind is positioned behind us, then ride the air current over the tree line and depart the lake. (This take off is more than academic, it is a personal work of art; the true mark of a man in love with his work.)

I am instructed to fly the airplane to Saratoga Lake; there I will proceed with my first water landing and take off.

We circle the lake to get an idea of wind, water and traffic conditions, both on and off the water.

Lou turns to me. "Give it a try."

I proceed, and revert to what I know; knowledge that is strictly used for land-based aircraft. With a stabilized approach, I continue toward the water. As I lose altitude I realize there is little, if any, reference to the proximity of the water's surface. Toward the later part of the approach I find myself looking for boat traffic or anything else to use as a point of reference. In spite of my efforts, I am not that displeased with the actual touchdown.

Once on the water, Lou instructs me to reduce power and hold the control wheel full back. The airplane decelerates rapidly and settles into the water. Once in the water, the wave we have made on landing catches up to gently raise the entire airplane, starting with the aft part of the floats, before settling back into the water.

He explains: what I have done is actually wrong, never try and guess where the surface of the water is, and do not try and find it. Water can feel like cement if contacted incorrectly. Lou motions me to start a take-off run as far away from surface traffic as possible, always watching for the occasional operator who has the desire to race the airplane, "They will be losers in more than ways than one."

I am to perform the next take off.

The amount of drag produced by the water is not fully appreciated until one actually performs the take-off. Double-checking the water rudder in the up position, I apply full power while holding the control wheel full aft. As the nose rises, I lose most of my forward visibility. I hold this attitude until the airplane reaches a point where further acceleration is impossible. It is at this point I find that just pushing the wheel forward will not necessarily place the airplane on the step; it takes a little practice. Once on the step, I continue the take-off and return for another water landing.

Lou proceeds with the next landing. Approaching the lake, Lou turns to me and then to our rear seat passenger, "Each water landing should almost be a surprise. That is, one never knows where the water really is." He continues with his conversation while looking at the shoreline through the side window behind me. I think, "if he doesn't watch where we are going, the touchdown won't be the only surprise". He is using the shoreline and gauging the attitude of the airplane while at the same time checking our altitude loss with judicious use of power.

I keep looking out the windshield, and then out the side of the airplane at the water below, then back to Lou, who at this time is the calmest person on board. We gently touch the surface of the water and skim across the small waves; at this point Lou adds more power to stay on top of the water until clear of all boats. I can feel a huge grin come over my face; looking at Lou he returns the smile.

We return to Round Lake where I try his technique, which results in two more huge grins.

Chuck's Aeronca float plane seats two in tandem. His take-off and landing techniques are very similar, however, being more maneuverable due to its size results in a slightly different ride than in the Cessna. The smaller lake to the northeast hosts enough room for a few fishermen in a few small rowboats. Approaching from the northeast, he side-slips the airplane over the marshland between the shore and the water; the floats brush the tall grass at the water's edge, and he performs a touch-and-go landing on one float. This is acknowledged by a casual wave from the occupant of one of the fishing boats. Once airborne again, he proceeds to hop over the treeline between the two bodies of water and land on the main lake. To some, this might prove slightly intimidating; to others it is a good time.

For the remainder of the spring, summer and well into the fall, there is more activity than anyone could have predicted. A typical day might see several airplanes in the pattern for the 2,300-foot gravel runway, while adjacent to us two or more float planes use the lake. Our flight schedule is busy enough to keep three Cessna 150's, a 172, and two floatplanes along with an equal amount of instructors busy from early morning until sunset, seven days a week. I never find time to finish my water rating.

Toward the end of October, we are all looking forward to the winter and some breathing room.

Don and Lou, although equally pleased, seem to sense that this will not last forever. They are right. The closing of the second season witnesses a dramatic economic slow down. We are not alone, for the whole industry is feeling the effects. Many full-time flying positions are abolished. The more fortunate positions continue on a part-time basis as did my own. Much like other small airports do, Round Lake operates on a day-to-day basis.

Stopping by the operation one afternoon, I engage in conversation with Don. He looks strangely tired; even with our jokes and reminiscing, it is obviously an effort for him to smile. Half-way into our conversation, he inquires about any interest I might have in purchasing Loudon Aircraft, "It is a good business for one man, Dick can perform your maintenance." He proceeds to inform me of the flying time on each airplane, which engine would be due for overhaul, and what AD notes have been complied with. With the slow economic picture, I have no idea where I could get funding, which is a sobering thought for both of us. I respectfully decline.

I feel something is missing; something not associated with my lack of purchasing his business. It goes beyond the obvious lack of energy and enthusiastic gestures so familiar of this man who has enjoyed a lifetime love affair with his flying. I sadly realize he has lost his spirit. Although having my suspicions, it is not until the following day that I become knowledgeable of his serious illness.

Three months later I receive a phone call from a former student explaining that Don has been hospitalized with a possible brain tumor behind one eye. Two days later I arrive at the hospital. As Dick Waterman and I step into his room, all is too apparent.

Under the given circumstances, and the fact that he had moved his operation twice, his spirits are good and he talks only of Loudon Airport. He still insists he could make a living with his latest endeavor in aerial spraying and of course his maintenance shop. I think this part of the conversation is more for our benefit than his. I find the conversation, at least on my part, difficult to keep going. In great gesture, it is suggested that when he gets out we get together and polish off a bottle of TulemorDew, his favorite whiskey.

"Well fellas, if I don't make it save it and drink on my grave, I'll still enjoy it." With that he musters a weak laugh; for me it is a battle to keep a smile on my face. Don passed away two days later.

Kenney Derringer, learned to fly at Loudon. His father also instructed. Earning his ratings he flew as instructor for Don and is now chief pilot for a Fixed Base Operator at Albany.

Richard Waterman, worked in maintenance at Loudon, he is now lead mechanic for a leading regional airline based in Upstate New York.

Ryan Morehead, started flying at Loudon, after earning his ratings became an instructor for Don and later he flies large corporate multi-engine aircraft.

Richard Ellington, performed engine maintenance for Don and now operates his own shop and FBO in Schenectady.

Bill Wallingford; started flying at Loudon, flew as an instructor for Don, and is now corporate pilot for an area-based contractor.

Myself included, these are the six pallbearers who carry Don's casket.

Engaged in conversation, we reminisce about the Loudon days, and the different aircraft we had flown for Don. The conversation proves almost endless. We discuss some of the many people he had known; including some well-known celebrities with whom he had come in contact through aviation.

One celebrity, a popular ventriloquist, (30) entertained at a local theater. While in the area he took flying lessons at Loudon Airport. One afternoon, from the trunk of his automobile he produced his man-made partner and gave us an impromptu private showing.

Another celebrity was a well known actor, (31) had flown his own Aztec into town while on tour. During the daytime, he gave airplane rides to some of the children from a local children's hospital. Before departing, he made it a point to stop by the airport over an hour prior to his departure just to engage in some hangar flying. He and Don held all our interest as they discussed flying some of the older airplanes. He told how he was presented the keys to his Aztec by his good friend, William T. Piper; founder of Piper Aircraft.

With all the flying we do with so many different students it is sometimes difficult to find time to fill out our logbooks; however, Don knew the names of every student each of us flew with. We laughed when the new regulations came about that required all instructors to keep track of their time flown with each student for currency requirements. Don was so far behind that he gathered all his paper notes and with the thickest logbook he could find, entered his time starting at the last page and worked forward to the first. He soon gave this job to his two oldest daughters.

No one knew how much flight time Don really had. He just loved to fly. Whether he logged it or not was not important to him. Among the six of us we try estimating the time he spent in the air, and it soon becomes apparent no one knows; not even Don.

Today we bury one of our own. Sadly, as each one of us say-goodbye to a friend, I think how much is owed to that little airport in Cohoes, New York, and to the man who ran it.

Chapter Eleven

Period of Adjustment

An impromptu meeting in the ground schoolroom finds me listening more than participating in a conversation among some of the local pilots, including some relatively new flight instructors, one of whom used to be associated directly with the operation. I am openly referred to as the "instructor from the old school". Although not exactly meant in a complimentary fashion, I find it amusing.

The FAA has virtually rewritten the regulations and requirements for every pilot license and rating. Once implemented, the transition is projected to be complete in approximately twenty-four calendar months. In the meantime, each licensed school will be required to operate using two sets of regulations for each license until the transition is complete.

A grandfather clause will allow those students presently enrolled to complete their courses within this time period. Enrollment after a certain date will automatically require enrollment under the new regulations. Also included are periodic flight checks for non-commercial pilots and changes in flight school operations. This challenge is not being graciously accepted by the industry.

As the conversation continues, I look around the room; I am the only witness to the usual huff and puff associated with these conversations, but once again target, " It will be interesting to see how an old school flight instructor used to dirt runways and old airplanes will adjust to these new regs!" Most of these pilots received their training in more sterile conditions than I, not to mention more modern airplanes and much better facilities to operate from. They have been spoiled, which probably explains their attitude; however, regulation changes have never changed basic piloting techniques. I just smile.

Retiring to my office for a cigarette before my next flight, I realize that my position as chief flight instructor is still under scrutiny.

Raymond Brown, my student for this hour, is checking the pattern for other traffic as we turn around and proceed with a take-off on runway 36 at Poestenkill. It still measures 2,800 feet long, sits in a bowl surrounded by trees and hills with power lines at both ends; and just for flavor, a swamp to the west side of the runway. Time has brought only two major differences to this airport- a paved runway, and taller trees.

Once airborne to the north, our flight path takes us over the familiar houses at near roof top altitude and then, just beyond that, the terrain drops off, exposing a large farm. Clearing the traffic pattern, we head toward the Tomahannock Reservoir and the practice area.

After executing some maneuvers enroute, I retrieve the hood from the rear seat of the Cherokee 140 and hand it to Ray. I direct him to fly a few turns and climbs before placing the aircraft into some unusual attitudes. Then relinquishing the controls, I observe his ability to recover. For the final maneuver, I place the aircraft in a slight nose down left turn, a set up for what is appropriately named the graveyard spiral.

"Ok Raymond, the airplane is yours."

His attempt at recovery is slow; he allows the airplane to gain more speed while increasing the bank, which results in a greater loss of attitude before reducing power. After prompting him twice, I take over the controls, with the command, "I got it."

His disorientation has lead to confusion and fright; he seems unable to relinquish the controls. The airspeed is starting to get dangerously high, "Let got of the controls!" The air rushing past the airframe is getting louder by the moment; we are now in a very critical condition where a recovery must be made. His grip on the controls finally prompts me to jab my elbow into his right arm, "Let go". I am starting to over-power him and continue the recovery when I feel something snap.

The left and right control wheels are now turned in opposite directions, "Take the hood off."

It is at this moment when he finally releases his grip on the wheel. I carefully finish the recovery using only rudder and elevator.

Once back in level flight, I catch my breath and assess the situation. This is one of the strangest situations I have ever seen; both control wheels remain turned in opposite directions. Very slightly, I try turning each one- without results; I have lost the use of the ailerons. Fortunately they have streamlined themselves and are now in the neutral position.

A look of absolute horror comes over Ray's face, "What do we do now?"

"I guess we are going to have to hang on and fly Raymond."

Fortunately the winds are light today; I make the return flight home and an uneventful landing using only the rudder, elevator and power for control.

Examination revels the chain connecting the two control wheel sprockets located behind the instrument panel has become dislodged, rendering control of the ailerons useless.

After crawling under the instrument panel to see for myself, I find it incredibly hard to believe any one man could be that strong. By this time a few local pilots have gathered around the airplane, mostly out of curiosity. Crawling back out of the airplane, I decide to arrange for maintenance and a substitute aircraft supplied for the day's schedule.

After conversing with Ray, one of the flight instructors from this morning actually enters the airplane to examine firsthand the position of both control wheels, "I have never seen anything like this before; I guess some people don't know their own strength."

Looking at me he continues, "Say, just exactly how did you fly this thing?"

Indulging myself in the moment I reply, "Old school."

The following morning finds me in conversation with the Commanding Officer of the Navy ROTC group, a Captain Bradford, tall with an athletic physique complimented by his uniform. During our discussion, he informs me of his transfer, and introduces his replacement,

Lt. Simpson. Simpson is a tall and thin man with dark hair and matching mustache, very much the pilot type, and similar in age; 33.

After a brief meeting, Bradford excuses himself, leaving just the two of us on the ramp, thereby allowing us to engage our selves in some "hangar flying." His last assignment was captain on a P-3 Orion, subchaser. He expresses his desires to do well in this new assignment, at which point I inform him that I too have just started my position. With that, we head over to one of the trainers. After a brief introduction to the airplane, we decide to take a flight, which proves to be the catalyst for the friendship that ensues between us.

The program starts in September with fifteen students all hand-picked by Simpson. Flights are scheduled during the week, and ground school sessions are on weeknights. Each student is starting from scratch; I do not have to teach over any other instructor's work, which is a great advantage. Simpson hands me the curriculum; "This is basically what we want." We compare his curriculum to that of the FAA, since it is within the limits of present regulations; we have time before the new changes take effect.

The curriculum is basic, with reasonable requirements for completion of each lesson, while leaving room for the instructor to work. Although it is a civilian curriculum, the guidelines have a more military approach regarding each progress check. Normally, a failed progress check means more instruction until the proficiency level is satisfactory; with this curriculum, it could mean the end of a pilot's career. This is designed to keep those involved on their toes; including Simpson and myself.

The flight course is conducted during the junior year, with application to the U.S, Naval Academy at Pensacola during the senior year. Each of these students is enrolled in an aeronautical engineering course at a local college and probably knows more about statistics and theory than I do. However, my job is teaching the practical application; which sometimes does not always follow the written word. So the training begins.

I decided to raise the level of acceptance higher than the curriculum; to accomplish this I must train accordingly. By the end of the third hour, each student is well versed in stalls from different configurations, as well as spin entries and recoveries. Greater emphasis is placed on take-offs and accuracy landings, including crosswind techniques. Simulated forced landings are accomplished with the mixture control placed in the idle cut-off position, rendering the throttle useless. These are practiced to touchdown; with the propeller wind milling until just before landing, adding a little more realism to the maneuver.

I apply the same level of acceptance for their basic instrument flying. As an added attraction, I take the time to teach maneuvers not normally found in a manual, such as recovery from partial inverted positions, and even a modified wing over for example.

Using these same techniques with all my students occasionally brings interesting comments and questionable looks from the local pilot population about my approach to instructing.

Periodic meetings find the lieutenant and I discussing the progress of each student. While complimenting him on his choice of students, with a smile, I refer to him as the guru of new pilots and a judge of fine whiskey. This always produces a good laugh.

Simpson asks. "What about their first solo?" I inform him that each one makes three-take-offs and landings, while I watch.

He smile and replies; "That is a hellava time to find out you forgot to teach them something!" I have to agree with that statement.

The results of the first year prove only two students rejected, one for physical reasons, the other for academic standing.

The third, and final year of the program, the curriculum is cut from 35 to 15 hours of flight, with only seven students enrolled instead of the usual fifteen. The only requirement is for a first solo, with the remainder of the training accomplished at Pensacola.

All is going well with the exception of one student. Gary is much quieter than his colleagues, and at times seems almost removed from them. He is not lazy; his performance is good when he chooses for it to be so. Speaking to him, he cowers similarly to that of a dog when being scolded, while his face turns almost completely red. This leads to cajoling, asking, commanding and sometimes almost pleading with him to shape up. With some anger in my voice I comment, "Gary, I know you can do this. My question is: do you want to?"

To this he just nods his head. The closer we get

to completion, the poorer his performance becomes. Simpson and I meet. We find it hard to believe both of us could have misjudged the same individual this poorly. Gary has one hour left; it is decided to let him finish that hour, resulting in an unsatisfactory progress check. The Navy will take care of the rest.

The next morning Gary arrives for his lesson.

"OK Gary, let's go shoot some landings." After three take-offs and landings, I direct him to park the machine.

Sitting in my office he reminds me of one who has been sentenced to a beheading, waiting for the axe to fall and end his misery.

"Talk to me Gary!"

He replies "What?"

Very quietly I ask him again. "Say something."

"I have to pass this course, otherwise everyone will think less of me, and I gotta pass."

I become quite angry, "This operation and my reputation are good because I have made them that way, not because someone else thought it would be a good idea." I pause briefly with a thought, and then explain that both are real and I am not about to gamble either one on his possible career, considering the quality of his performance.

"Sometimes Gary, a little moxie goes a long way."

A look of determination comes over his face, which causes me to make a proposal, "Three perfect take-off's and landings, otherwise forget it."

He meets the challenge; although not outwardly showing it, I am very pleased.

"Now, I want the next three landings to be exactly

adjacent to where the edge of the taxiway meets the runway. Got it?" I exit the airplane. Standing by the side of the runway, I watch as he aborts his first take-off. After the airplane comes to a stop, I observe closely, briefly wondering to myself if he has chosen to quit, or if he has forgotten something. I watch closely as he reaches overhead to the latch on the door. This he had forgotten to do prior to take-off. He has successfully handled this potential problem exactly as it should be handled. As he turns around to taxi back for another take-off I know all will go well, his next three landings prove that. Gary left the airport a different person. I call Lt. Simpson to inform him Gary's flight training is finished and add that he has satisfactorily completed his basic flight training.

Later that year, after visiting Simpson, he informs me all is well with the students, except Gary. On my way out, I notice Gary sitting at a long study table shared by several students. As I speak, I quickly realize this is not the real Gary. His face speaks of failure, as does his speech. I can feel my face turning red as I speak, "Gary, didn't you learn anything?" To add to my anger I feel saddened by what I see, and leave the room. It will be some time before I ever hear of him again.

The mid November morning leaves a light coating of snow only on the aircraft and grassy areas. After preheating and deicing the airplane, we engage in a tug of war to get the main gear out of the recess in the grass and onto the pavement. Once in the airplane, my student starts his routine with the checklist in preparation for this morning's flight, which is expected to be routine.

The north, northwest winds favor runway 36, and our weather this morning favors us with high ceilings and good visibility. Just before our take-off roll, I make mention the cabin heater is working well, "Let's go for a ride."

Take-off appears normal, rotation executed at the proper location and airspeed. With an altitude gain of approximately fifteen feet, our comfortable cabin is interrupted with a deafening silence, we have lost power. I immediately put the aircraft back on what runway is left. With the end of the runway and swamp approaching rapidly I apply heavy braking, while trying not to lock up a wheel. My actions result with the nose gear on the end of the runway just before the overrun preceding the swamp.

I turn to my student, "You OK Jack?"

"Yeah, I think so." As we deplane from our warm cabin I make mention of the fact that if there are any brakes left on the airplane, I am not the one to blame. After pushing the airplane onto the ramp, I summon our mechanic, Hammed.

He is a soft-spoken man of slight build of Middle Eastern decent. He is rarely known to start a conversation. He looks at the airplane without saying a word.

"Hammed, would you like to know what happened?" He looks at me as if I should know that he knows I am going to tell him anyway.

"It swallowed something it did not like." With that, we both question all possibilities, including fuel contamination. After draining each sump again, the fuel samples seem fine.

After a few minutes, Hammed tries starting the engine. Balky at first, it does start, after several moments of operation it smoothes out, even the magneto check seem normal.

"Ok, sir you can fly the airplane now, I think it was moisture."

Ever since my arrival at Poestenkill, I have been trying to get him into an airplane; I have always been more comfortable with a mechanic who will ride behind his own work. I thank him and ask which seat he is going to occupy during the test flight.

"No-no-no-no-no, this is quite alright, I am busy today."

I reply, "First of all, if this thing quit just over those trees, I would be talking to you from someone's kitchen. Second; I would feel much better if we took a closer look at the air intake before passing judgment on the airworthiness of this airplane. Third, if you will not ride behind your own work, neither will I."

"No sir, this time I do not think you will have another *amerjensee.*"

"Another what?" After he repeats himself several times, the lineman taps me on the shoulder and informs me that the word is "emergency"

Slightly frustrated, we look again. The air intake line has an air filter located behind the landing light. I ask if water can get passed the filter for any reason. With a questionable look on his face, he raises his shoulders in what looks like an effort to touch his ears.

The air intake hose has a low point between the air filter and the carburetor. After removal, there is visible moisture inside the line.

We continue investigating, looking for a reasonable explanation; last night the main gear was parked in the grass, which is considerably lower than the pavement on the ramp, where the nose wheel had been parked. During the driving rain the previous night, water passed through the air filter and collected inside the air intake hose. With the passage of the cold front, everything froze, including the water that had collected inside the intake hose. During deicing and engine preheating, the ice melted. Once the engine was started, the residual heat kept the water from refreezing. As the airplane rotated for take-off, the water was ingested into the carburetor. The rest is history. With that, we include a closer look into the air intake hose on each flight.

Contending with the regulation changes brings another series of events. There are disagreements not only concerning the graduation approval for each course, but also upon each school inspection. The examining inspectors cannot agree which grading system to use for each lesson. Some inspectors want a grading system using numbers, others letters, while others want words such as; satisfactory or unsatisfactory. Upon concluding each school inspection, I receive a letter explaining what changes are to be made in our grading system. During the next inspection, the entire scenario is repeated, making for some interesting paperwork.

The instructor's endorsement of each student's solo cross-country flights also proves a memorable event with one of the inspectors. We disagree on the usage of one word; according to him I am in violation of said regulation. While reading aloud the regulation in question, I point out there is no provision or standardization for confirming any proper word usage, only an instructor's endorsement confirming preparedness of the student for each event.

We are arguing over an interpretation of the regulation. The longer the phone conversation lasts, the louder we both get. The ensuing argument ends as we hang up simultaneously. Later that morning I receive a call from the head of the local office confirming there is nothing in writing, merely a suggestion for compliance.

To add substance to our lives, periodically, a few of the local residents stop in and loudly express their displeasure with the operation, some just to make noise. One individual actually threatens disastrous damage to the airplanes should one fly over his house one more time. During this ridiculous conversation, his breath is evidence of his state of non-sobriety, leaving me wondering if he could inflict any damage to anyone other than himself. On one visit, I actually show him a photograph of the property prior to his house being built. The photo was taken from one of our airplanes. Staring at the photograph, he keeps muttering about the inability to see his house; I interrupt, "That is because it is not in the picture." Although his visits are infrequent, they are memorable.

In spite of our trials and tribulations, we manage to enjoy a lighter side.

A spot-landing contest is organized strictly for our own pilots. Using some lime we mark a white line across the runway near the north taxiway. Here we place randomly chosen judges to document each landing. The contest is open to student, and private and commercial pilots. Flight instructors are excluded. Each pilot buys a 50/50 ticket to enter the contest, with all participants celebrated at the barbeque that follows. One of my own students won first place.

This is probably the smallest airport in history to ever host an air show. Lacking such acts as the Blue Angels, or Thunderbirds due to airspace restrictions, the air show is as complete as any air show one could imagine, and probably the biggest single event ever held in the town of Poestenkill. One particular act flown at most air shows is the flying farmer act. A well-known local pilot dresses up as a farmer and he is left alone in a supposedly runaway airplane; his routine is to convince the audience of his total lack of airmanship. The narrator of the show adds to the illusion. After some interesting maneuvers, his finale includes landing the airplane dead stick in front of the audience, who by now realizes this is just a good act.

In our show, we depict a grandmother about to embark on her first flight, supposedly left alone in a runaway airplane. I do not mind the flight routine; however, I look a little ridiculous wearing a polka-dotted dress and a straw hat that are both accented by a pocket book and my mustache.

Another change at the airport, is the introduction of Piper's new purpose built, low wing two-place trainer.

Its design is rather unique; low wing, a bubble canopy with the most noticeable difference being the high "T" tail design (32). Requiring only 100 hp means less fuel consumption, and fewer seats means lower insurance premiums. The plane is called the Tomahawk.

This afternoon, I discuss the new trainer with, Jeff Marconi, (an engineer by profession, methodical and quiet by nature), looking over his glasses halfway down his nose. He nods his head in acknowledgement of the conversation, while sitting with his feet on the desk near the window.

Chris Mallory, a well-educated quick witted businessman, enjoys a good laugh as much as he enjoys teaching aerobatics in his own plane (which he engages in frequently). First standing and then walking back and forth in the office while lighting a cigarette, he is very much part of our discussion concerning the new airplane.

Although similarly qualified, the reactions of each flight instructor are true to their personalities. Jeff, just smiles, shrugs his shoulders and says flatly "Ok, whatever."

Chris exclaims. "Great, can't wait to see what Piper does with this one."

I have to admit, I am a little curious myself.

Our first Tomahawk arrives late one summer afternoon. The airplane is furnished with a very professionally made white vinyl hardcover flight manual. The contents include aircraft specifications, full color photographs and meticulously illustrated performance graphs, all arranged in alphabetical order in a three-ringed format for easy addition of revisions.

After consulting the manual, I am off for a familiarization flight. The airplane has a little quicker control response, and while still quite controllable, the stall characteristics are more pronounced and without hesitation as compare to the Cherokee.

Since the airplane is designed mainly as a trainer, I proceed to engage the aircraft in a spin. The response is quick in the first half turn; in fact it almost appears to be slightly inverted at that point. I continue one more turn with the recovery just as responsive as the entry.

Later that afternoon, I review the VCR tape that came with the airplane. Technically, in the first half turn of the spin the airplane is inverted, with the nose 110 degrees below the horizon, returning to 60 degrees below the horizon by the completion of the first turn. It will be interesting to see how this airplane is received.

A few days later, I discuss the new Tomahawk with Chris Mallory. After answering a few of his questions, I inform him the airplane is quite controllable, easy to fly and a piece of cake to spin.

A few moments later, I address Jeff on the ramp and ask of Chris's whereabouts. He informs me Chris has just departed with one of his students in the Tomahawk.

"He never let me finish our conversation."

Jeff looks at me inquisitively, "I didn't mention to him the machine will go inverted in the first half turn of a spin." We both chuckle, as we both know exactly what Chris is going to do.

Returning from a flight late that day, I approach the

Tomahawk parked on the ramp from behind. There, draped across the brace bar inside the rear window is the flight manual. On the floor in front of the instructor's seat is the checklist. I immediately seek out Chris's whereabouts.

During our discussion, he describes his flight. Chris forced the airplane into a spin, which hastened the entry to the inverted position. After applying full opposite rudder to stop the rotation, he then rather abruptly applied full nose down elevator to stop the stall. This resulted in a negative G loading on the airplane. Anything not tied down inside the airplane was actually thrown against the ceiling of the cabin, resulting in some untidy housekeeping. As I walk into the office, I overheard his student comment; "Let's not do that again ok?"

I look at Chris as we both laugh. "Interesting airplane isn't it Chris?'

An early fall morning finds me in my office opening the morning mail, which includes the latest revisions for my airway manual and a letter from the FAA in Washington. There is a proposal to make Albany County Airport a Terminal Control Area (33). Restricting that airspace for use only by aircraft using the facilities at Albany. This will require a special clearance to operate in this airspace at less than 7,000 feet, and within 20 miles of the facility. Drastically increasing its present geographic area. As I look at the airspace restriction, its eastern jurisdiction includes a good portion of my practice area. The same authority that granted the flight school operating certificate with authorized practice area now wants to restrict the same airspace for traffic using

Albany Airport. This will mean I won't be able to comply
with the new flight school regulations. A meeting will be
held at the Niskayuna High School; I decided to attend.

Entering the auditorium, it is obvious that emotions
are running high. The meeting, which is already in
progress, bears a strange resemblance to a lynching; in
this case the FAA representative from Washington who is
conducting the meeting is the object of ill attention. The
operators and pilots already knee-deep in transitions over
the new regulations, have yet another one to contend with.
The representative is displaying great discipline while
listening to the screaming voices and harsh complaints
and trying to answer all questions in a dignified manner.

On the wall behind our representative is a blow-up
facsimile of the aerial chart for Albany. After listening
to several angry complaints from the microphone-
equipped podium supplied for tonight's meeting, I half-
heartedly raise my hand in what I think to be a seemingly
unnoticeable gesture. Suddenly a loud voice behind me
says, "Common Eddie, get up there and tell 'em!" My
first reaction is to find a place to hide, however that is
impossible.

I approach the podium and introduce myself, at the
same time producing a letter I have written addressed to
the FAA regarding tonight's subject.

I nervously begin by locating Poestenkill (10 miles
east-southeast of Albany) on his projected chart for
confirmation. My only hope is to push the safety issue as
it pertains to the school's operation. I proceed to explain.
"First, the extension of the TCA, as proposed, restricts us

from the airspace now used for our practice area. Second, this will require traveling a considerable distance to find suitable airspace to safely perform the air work required for each course, adding to the cost of each flight. Thirdly, performing these maneuvers underneath the TCA will place the aircraft at an unsafe altitude due to their nature." I am trying to be professional, calm, cautious and articulate in a room that has become so quiet I can almost hear myself perspire.

In another effort to produce more evidence against the change in regulations, I proceed to explain in detail the three incidences I had been involved in during the past fourteen months, each one requiring evasive action to prevent a possible collision. The first, a Learjet while being radar-vectored, flew through the traffic pattern at Poestenkill, which is not in Albany's jurisdiction. Additionally, shortly after receiving a clearance to land on runway 19 at Albany, I was issued a clearance for an immediate go-around; looking underneath me, a 727 had just touched down on the runway. The third incident occurred after being cleared for an instrument approach to runway 28 at Albany from approach control, a King Air flying behind me was cleared to land on the same runway, then proceeded to pass just overhead, and slightly to my right. Interestingly enough, I was in the process of taking an annual flight check; the right seat occupant was an FAA inspector.

I conclude with an explanation that all individuals involved in these incidents are properly licensed and operating aircraft with proper equipment thus satisfying the criteria for operating in a TCA. (Even though none existed at the time)

"If the equipment on the airport or the aircraft or personnel requirements is not going to change, I do not see how a TCA is going to make aviation around Albany any safer." I presented a copy of this letter to the representative, then quietly and swiftly leave the room.

The next few weeks afford a return to normalcy, while enabling me to maintain a low profile. One morning, while in discussion with another pilot, I am informed of a person-to-person long distance phone call for me. I ask, "From whom?"

"It's Washington." I laugh while rephrasing the question.

"The FAA from Washington, they want to speak to you."

Half laughing I reply, "Well, it's about time."

Jeff and Chris stand by the office door listening intently as I half-heartedly answer the phone. The voice on the other end asks for me in person, "This is he." To my surprise, it is FAA headquarters, Washington D.C. After a long discussion I am informed that my letter had provided enough information to postpone the implementation of a TCA until further investigation is complete. I inform my listeners of the conversation; there is a huge sigh of relief just prior to several bursts of cheering, the loudest coming from Jeff.

Through the window I watch the early morning rain make small puddles on the ramp. It is one of those mornings when the chill in the air makes a good cup of coffee seem great and a quiet atmosphere lures one to indulge in some private thoughts.

Although very pleased with the results of the postponement of the TCA, I know it is inevitable. However, today is not the day to waste time worrying.

I am still referred to as the old school flight instructor, more affectionately I might add. Our reputation as a good flight school has grown as well as our student population; with advertisement largely by word of mouth.

I have had our mechanic, Hammed, in enough airplanes I have accused him of building up his frequent flyer miles.

Lt. Simpson has finished his tour of duty. We have had great success; only two have not graduated into Pensacola, one with a medical condition, the other a scholastic shortcoming. Simpson's next tour of duty is Pensacola, along with his promotion. (34)

We have made it through the change-over in the regulations and are now operating under one set of rules; this alone is a relief. Adding to this thought, the quality of our graduates is second to none.

Even the local residents have a different viewpoint, thanks in part to our air show; our most outspoken opponent actually joined me for several beers following the show. I had one, he had the rest.

There are now two Tomahawks in the flight-training program, the airplane being well received by all. Interestingly, spins are no longer considered a maneuver performed by someone else.

Closing the top drawer to the filling cabinet and thinking, "I am still alone," in relief, I mutter one thought out loud, "I guess we have finally made it though that period of adjustment."

"We certainly did," an unexpected voice responds.

Startled, I turn around to see the source of the comment. In full dress Navy uniform, including pilot's wings, proudly stands Gary.

Chapter Twelve

F Stands for Surprise

The short flight from Poestenkill, where I am also the chief pilot for the charter operation, has me arriving at the only FBO at Albany Airport. I often find myself in the company of several other pilots from corporations and other charter companies. It is here, in the early morning, where most of our predawn flights originate.

The pilot briefing areas are a good source of information pertaining to our business, or place just to exchange stories. Once again, my attempt to simultaneously yawn and drink my first coffee of the day is unsuccessful.

Sitting across the table from me is Tom Covington, a charter pilot based in Schenectady. Our individual flights are scheduled to depart Albany at 05:30 am. His wavy blonde hair shows signs of recent grooming, while his eyes reflect the early morning hour behind the smoke rising from his pipe.

"How many oh-dark-thirty take-offs have you had this week?"

"I'm not sure; I think I have slept through most of them."

We both chuckle on my reply. Today Tom is off to Newark and I am headed for LaGuardia. We rarely fly the same route each day; every flight is different, with its own peculiarities. Add in a little weather, and things can prove interesting.

On good weather days, the countryside is a delight-
ful sight at sunrise. On other flights, I will lose sight of the
ground shortly after take-off, spend the rest of the flight
solely engaged in the instrument panel until my next
glimpse of terra firma seconds before touchdown. This requires greater concentration and skill, and with single pilot
operations, leaves one in need of some rest afterward.

Many of the more modern facilities offer lounge
chairs and quiet rooms for the pilots to rest, making
them a welcomed sight for arriving pilots. On numerous
occasions, due to weather or traffic, my only other wish is
for a good co-pilot.

This morning, being number thirty-three for
departure from LaGuardia could almost be considered a
miracle, considering my original number was six. Like all
major hubs, where all flights are scheduled to depart and
arrive at the same time, major aeronautical traffic jams
result. I have had much higher numbers than this for the
same departure. Inclement weather at either end makes
the delays seem endless.

Closing the cover on my Jeppeson Airway Manual,
I enjoy the beautiful cloudless day as I make my way
northward from LaGuardia to home base in the newest
addition to the fleet, the latest F Model Aztec.

Not all airports are as glamorous or congested as
LaGuardia. Today I have been scheduled to fly three
people to a small airport in mid-state New York. Checking
the appropriate chart, it indicates a seasonal airport, and
I explain to all concerned that this might not be a good
place to land this early in the spring.

There are three passengers. Louie who is of short stature, dressed rather expensively and obviously in charge of this entourage. He resembles an underworld character straight from Hollywood. Joey is as tall as Louie is short, dressed similarly and bearing a strong resemblance to a bodyguard. The third member is Larry; a typical thin, quiet, bi-focal laden accountant type. This self-appointed panel of aviation experts is assuring that with me the pilot, all will be well, and there is nothing to be concerned about. With tongue in check I agree to take the trip. I stipulate however that there are no guarantees. A departure to Canandaigua, New York is under way.

My altitude puts me in and out of the clouds for most of the trip. Approaching Rochester, the clouds become more overcast and typically laden with the snow blown in off the lakes. Once in contact with Rochester Approach, I request a let down and possible radar back up to our destination. Clearing the bottom of the clouds, the controller complies with my request;

"Aztec 526, the airport is one o'clock two miles… one o'clock mile and a half… half mile… the airport should be coming up just to the right of your nose."

I start a right bank and look over the wing and there it is.

I estimate the runway length at 1,500 feet, half of which is under water. The ducks that are not swimming on the runway I am confident are perched inside the hangar adjacent to it.

"There it is folks."

After gawking momentarily, the comments ensue,

"There is what?"

I reply, "The airport of destination."

After a brief moment of silence, which has allowed me to circle the runway, I receive the ultimate question, "Aren't you going to land?"

I explain that this airplane does not have webbed landing gear, and if I were good enough to get the airplane in without damaging it, we will have to wait for summer before I can get it out.

Then comes the ultimate statement; one I know I would not want to miss.

"Now hold on just one minute, I have a limousine that is going to pick us up here."

I explain that unless the driver is talking to the same controller I am, there is little chance of finding this place even from the ground.

"Hang on a second, I'll see if there is another airport around here we can use."

Trying to keep my composure, I contact the controller to advise him of our situation. Within a few moments, he has vectored me over to a more suitable airport.

Below me is a grassy north-south runway that sits snuggly at the bottom of a hill on the west side; a building on the east side supports a windsock indicating a direct crosswind from the west. I advise Rochester Approach, and then contact the advisory frequency for the airport below. A very slow voice responds as though he is giving a sight-seeing tour of an old farmhouse, "I suppose if you use some caution you should be alright, there are a few soft spots, not that bad though. West wind kicks up a bit. But we got machines around here like yours, should be ok."

I have a feeling this is going to be a long day.

I enter downwind to parallel the runway and size up the situation, and then proceed with the approach. The turbulence increases as I descend. On the later part of the final approach, the turbulence caused by the wind flowing over the hill on the west becomes so strong that the airplane becomes difficult to handle and warrants a go-around. On the departure, the turbulence is almost unbearable to the point that it actually frightens the passengers.

Once he catches his breath, Louie makes a statement, "Take me home, forget about this place!"

Once the airplane has settled down and is more man-ageable, I make an announcement, "Calm down, it's just a few bumps, you're all OK. We will take another look."

"You are going to do what?" It was at this point I wish I had a camera.

I explain, "First; I now have an idea of what to expect, second, at least there are no ducks swimming on the runway; and third, what are you going to do about the limousine?"

On the second approach, the wind had slackened a little, and I continue the approach down to the runway. Just after touchdown I roll through one "soft spot" causing a considerable volume of water to wash over the left side of the airplane. I add enough power to keep the airplane moving until we are parked on the only pavement on the airport, which is the apron next to a building.

As we deplane, the trio looks around in disbelief. There is no terminal with all the accoutrements, just your basic farm-country airport. Louie requests a phone; he is escorted to a coin box mounted on the wall next to the single restroom. Joey then occupies the rest room, while Larry, holding his briefcase with both hands, waits for his turn. I then survey the place. Two ancient stuffed chairs in the main room resemble furniture resurrected from the Salvation Army. One desk in the corner is a collection point for everything from old coffee cups to spark plugs, to cylinder heads for the Cessna, which I can see through the open door behind it.

The two men are the only occupants of this establishment, and are genuinely friendly and dressed in the traditional grease-soaked coveralls, in contrast to the four of us dressed in three-piece suits. One of them is looking at the Aztec parked on the ramp while the other seems to be the official greeter, "What brings you fellas to these parts?"

Louie answers, "I'd like to know the answer to that one myself. As soon as I get home, I will have a talk with my secretary."

Turning to me he admits, "Next time I will listen to you."

About 45 minutes later, the limousine arrives, driven by a very beautiful young lady with long auburn hair, wearing a well-tailored pin-stripe suit with a white ruffled blouse open enough to attract attention. I approach her as she stands next to one of the mud puddles in the parking lot. During our brief discussion, she tells me of the difficulty in finding this place, never knowing that such places actually existed. I smile, "Allow me to show you what is on the other side of that building."

"No thank you", she responds

I watch as the limousine departs. Returning to the office, I engage in a conversation with the occupants who by now have several questions regarding the airplane, the limousine, and in particular the driver. After about an hour's conversation, I ask to borrow an old flying magazine sitting on the work bench and proceed to the cleanest over-stuffed chair.

The limousine driver awakens me. In a very soft spoken voice she says, "Hello again, Louie insists you have something to eat before they depart." She hands me a Styrofoam container with a roast beef sandwich and a big cup of coffee.

Thanking her I ask, "Is this considered breakfast in bed around these parts?

"No, we serve duckling for that," she replies.

"I guess news travel fast around here."

Smiling she answers, "Yes it does."

I perform the pre take-off checklist on the apron; from here I keep the airplane moving briskly through the wet grass until into position for take-off. Once achieved, the take-off is performed academically; the return trip to Albany is uneventful.

The spring is celebrated by the initiation of frequent cargo flights to Charleston, West Virginia. The removal of the two seats behind the pilot is required to accommodate the freight. Since there are no passengers on these flights, the company of another pilot, or student who wishes to gain some experience and fly as co-pilot is always welcomed. Each of the flights plays host to different weather conditions, some good, while in other cases my logbook entries reflect some of the more interesting variations.

There is one flight that has earned a rather unusual entry. On this day, Jerry Madison, an advanced student of mine chooses to ride the right seat. Jerry is of medium height with jet-black hair and matching glasses that are complimented by his genuine smile and well-maintained handlebar mustache. He is known for his great technical vocabulary, and tasteful jokes; he is at all times a true gentleman.

Climbing to 8,000 feet along the airway southwest of Albany, we encounter light rain. At first, the ground is visible, but as the rain falls, adding more moisture to the lower altitudes, I know that soon we will be flying in solid cloud. I can hear other pilots reporting deteriorating weather along the route, which confirms my personal prediction. I ask center for 10, 000 feet in my search for smoother air.

There is a stereophonic, almost hypnotic drone of both engines in perfect synchronization with each other, and the engine instruments confirm to us the well being of each. The rain makes a light hissing sound as it hits the windshield and passes over the airframe on its way to the ground. Jerry is changing the station frequency for navigation to the next VOR, while I neatly fold the chart on my lap to expose the next leg of the airway leading to that station. At this moment there is a quiet contentment with our lives as we enjoy a true airspeed of 175 knots and a smooth ride.

Suddenly, there is a loud crash of metal hitting the airframe on the pilot's side of the aircraft just behind the passenger compartment. I immediately place both hands on the control wheel. The autopilot-disengage warning horn sounds as I disengage the autopilot. I have both feet firmly placed on the rudder pedals. My mind and heart are going faster than this airplane could ever fly. A mid air collision is a pilot's greatest fear; this can render control of an airplane totally impossible.

Both of our reactions are electric; checking and rechecking flight instruments, checking engine instruments and flight controls then rechecking again. Up to this point I still have control of the airplane, a big plus. All systems seem to be functioning properly. I take a quick glance at Jerry, whose face has a look that exemplifies both our thoughts; what did we hit? I briefly contemplate calling the Center to inform them of our predicament, but quickly change my mind. "What would I tell him, and how would I explain?" It is almost absurd to think someone would be illegally cloud busting at this altitude. Neither Center nor any aircraft on this frequency have reported communications problems. There are two pilots on board this airplane and we both heard something hit the airplane, but what? We are left without explanation.

We are still in the clouds and riding through light rain. I pull on my shirt that is damp with perspiration, while Jerry wipes his brow. This scenario that has taken mere seconds in time has seemed an eternity. It is now obvious we are not going to lose control of the airplane; I reach down and reengage the autopilot with a hand that is unbelievably steady given the circumstances. After a few more sighs of relief, we decide to inspect what we can from this vantage point. This is one of those rare moments in a pilot's life when he wishes he were on the ground.

After several moments of searching, I notice the obvious; something is missing from the inboard side of the left engine nacelle. There is usually a 4" round convex mirror that is attached to the aircraft at this location. This allows the pilot to visually monitor the position of the nose gear, and is used as a backup for the gear lights and the down and locked position of the gear handle. Obviously the airplane was painted after the mirror was installed, for all that remains is a 4" round patch of zinc chromate primer. After closer inspection, I do not see a hole for the attachment bolt that holds the mirror in place. Whatever method was used for the attachment has obviously failed.

"Look! The mirror is missing."

Jerry, looking at the last known position of the mirror and says, "I don't believe it. From the noise I thought we hit another airplane."

"Jerry, it looks to me as though we had a midair collision with our own parts." This is followed by a moment of silence. It is amazing just how fast one's mind and body can operate under such circumstances. I cannot find enough words in my vocabulary to describe my feeling of relief.

Jerry, who between us has the better vocabulary,

put his head in his hands and spoke quite precisely, "Holy shit!"

We both had a much-needed laugh.

After landing, we inspect the left side of the airplane. The departed mirror has removed a considerable amount of blue and gold paint from the vertical fin and rudder, no doubt a sentimental gesture.

"What do we put in the logbook for this one?" Jerry asks.

"How about; 'Miss you, wish you were here.' " This will prove to be only one of several interesting incidents before the year is through.

A leaking windshield takes its place as the next surprise. While waiting in Albany for the passage of an early morning snowstorm, approximately four inches of wet, heavy snow is left behind. The airplane sits for half a day while the melting of the snow allows water to accumulate in the channel connecting both halves of the windshield, and then freezes. The bottom of the channel is located behind the instrument panel directly above the electronic installation for the aircraft.

On climb out, the cabin heat melts the ice. I reach over to change navigation frequency on the number one radio, whereby I am witness to a very unusual event; water is trickling from between the number one and number two radios, and continues down the front of the entire electronics package before dispensing itself inside the throttle quadrant.

Maintenance removes both halves of the windshield in order to repair the leak. The water I had seen was small in proportion to what had leaked behind the instrument panel; all the electronics are removed and actually placed in ovens to cook in order to dry them sufficiently. The entire repair to the airplane takes two weeks.

While sipping on a fresh cup of coffee, our chief mechanic enters my office. Craig is six feet tall, thirtyish, with thinning hair on top of his head that is compromised by its overall length. As he quietly speaks, his nose lifts up his glasses to expose a generous grin underneath his mustache, "Chief, I don't think this is going to make your day."

I respond with a question, "Don't tell me, this has something to with one Aztec 62526?"

His smile quickly disappears as he hands me an AD note issued by the FAA on the F model Aztec.

The newer model has external counterbalances for the stabilator. These extend about one foot forward of the leading edge on either side of the tail surface, replacing the older style which was located inside the aft portion of the fuselage.

I initially have reservations about the new tail design, concerning its ability to handle ice, but practical applications prove my reservations baseless. However, routine inspections have found fatigue cracks on the connecting arms, serious enough to ground the airplane until proper repairs are completed. Enough airplanes are affected that parts are back-ordered for weeks. While exhaling smoke from a recently lit cigarette, Craig smiles sheepishly, "I did not know that the F stands for surprise."

I reply, " I sure hope this is the end of the surprises

with this airplane."

It is not.

During a six-month pilot proficiency check, I engage in an interesting conversation with Mark, the FAA check pilot, who also has considerable amount of time in Aztecs. While taxiing out to the runway, he mentions a recent accident involving an Aztec. According to information on hand, while on final approach, as the pilot lowered the flaps, the door popped open. The aircraft then rolled to the right and crashed, demolishing the airplane and leaving the pilot with serious injuries. Mark also states that the pilot had more time in Aztecs than I. I deposit this information in my personal memory bank, and continue with the flight.

The south ramp at Albany County Airport is a lonely place after dark. The Northwest wind makes the clear winter night seem even colder. I pull the kerosene heater to the end of the tailgate on the aging Ford wagon to preheat the aircraft's engines. I cannot stop shivering as the strong wind gusts pierce my clothing like a cold knife. Having landed here the night before in weather conditions that did not permit returning to home base, I am now retrieving the airplane in preparation of tomorrow's flight.

Standing on the right wing, I unlock the door and climb down and into a dark cold cabin. With the aid of a flashlight, I locate the checklist and read off each item in order; soon the engines are running, instrument lights illuminate the panel, radios are alive, and best of all, the cabin heater is making things a little more user-friendly.

Reaching to my right, I follow the normal procedure for closing and locking the door. I remove my gloves and place them on the right seat. For some reason, I adjust the curtain on the pilot's side window. Outside of aesthetics, they have no use to me. I listen to the automatic weather broadcast for Albany, while adjusting the altimeter and contacting the clearance delivery for my departure.

To the uninitiated, the sea of lights on the surface of an airport seem confusing and endless. In actuality, their presence makes navigating to and from the active runway much simpler. Many airports, such as Albany, also have lighted signs with arrows to aid in navigation to and from each. As I progress to the active runway, the lights on the aircraft reflect a cold, bare, lifeless stretch of pavement that lies between the blue taxiway lights. The half moon reflecting off the frozen snow on either side of the taxiway makes me shiver on this cold lonely night. I have no idea what made me think of this, but there was a time when pilots flew out of here with considerably less lighting and in open cockpit airplanes. Now just how lucky can one get?

At the end of the blue lights, I taxi into position between the white lights on runway 28; here I receive my clearance for take-off. One more glance at the instrument panel tells me that warning lights are out, so I advance the throttles to full power. As the propellers cut into the cold night air, acceleration and take-off are swift and positive. Once a good rate of climb is established, I reach down to the right of the throttle quadrant for the gear handle. As I release the lock and pull the handle up, there is an exploding sound followed by the loud rush of air from the right side of the airplane.

Simultaneously, the curtain has become detached from the left window and proceeds to wrap itself around my head making it impossible to see the instrument panel. I am startled, surprised and temporarily incapacitated.

In the process of grabbing at the curtain in a desperate attempt to remove it, one of the hooks that attaches the curtain to the window rakes itself across my forehead. Interestingly, the harder I struggle the less headway I gain until finally I am able to take part of the curtain off my head and throw it. Once I can see, my next job is to fly the airplane. I have only three hundred feet between the ground and myself. Looking to my right, I notice that the door has popped wide open.

Once I have the airplane back under control, I turn left and back onto the downwind side of the runway, while contacting the tower for a clearance to land. The noise is so great that I have difficulty hearing my clearance. So I keep my attention solely on flying to maintain the airplane at slow cruise. I do not know what to expect under this situation.

I am amazed that the door actually trails open more than a foot, and although I can reach over with one arm and close it, I cannot reset the locking mechanism even with both hands. It is getting colder by the second in the cabin and the rhythmic pumping of air over the right wing from each rotating propeller blade is raising havoc with my eardrums. I try changing power settings in an attempt to lessen the effects of the open door; none seem to work. There is a little more vibration than normal on the control wheel. I am not sure if the situation has some effect on the tail surfaces or perhaps I am just noticing this more.

I start my approach, base leg, gear down, and there is more discomfort than anything; I still remain very cautious. It is final approach and I reach for the flap handle suddenly remembering my conversation with Mark. I stop myself. I am not about to experiment with flaps and the opened door. I'm light, I do not have any passengers and there is one long runway. I keep power on almost to the runway, make some final corrections for the crosswind and execute a no flap landing.

After the landing roll, I turn off onto the nearest taxiway and stop. The chill that runs through my body is due to more than just cold air. The door itself is now resting against the jam; the sudden change in pressure not only removes the curtain, but also my chart and gloves, which I had placed on the seat next to me.

While regaining my composure, I notice the red light on the panel in front of me is lit, the placard underneath reading "door ajar". Later with some help, the door is jury rigged for the flight home and the aircraft grounded.

The next morning as I enter the shop, Craig greets me with his usual smile. With a slight laugh in his voice, pointing to his own forehead he comments, "Looks like she bopped you one."

"No Craig, it's called a curtain." With that we both laugh.

He requests me to sit inside the airplane and close the door; as I comply, I notice the interior of the door has been removed to expose the inner workings.

The door itself is approximately four feet wide, three feet tall with a curve on the top, which extends into the ceiling of the cabin allowing for cabin access. To close the door requires two hands. One hand holds the door handle in the full upright position, the other is used to physically close the door.

The handle is connected to a semicircular plate with two small arms. Attached to these arms are arm extensions made of flat metal bands that have been machine rolled along the sides for strength. One extends to the rear of the door, the other to the bottom. Once the door is placed in the closed position the handle is placed in the full forward or locked position. This action pushes the arm extensions, which in turn positions the locks or dead bolts into the door jam to hold the door closed and locked. Overhead is a smaller lock which simply provides a snug fit at the top. The front of the door holds a button and when pushed down operates a small rod that does nothing but open the switch for the "door ajar" light on the panel.

Once the door is closed, all seems normal until Craig yells to me to lean against it. At that point the door opens, triggering the door ajar light on the instrument panel. I must have had a perplexed look on my face as Craig requests a repeat performance, "Close the door again, then check the extension arms for each lock." I comply; this time as I lock the door, both arms actually bow, thus placing each lock only half way into the doorframe. The overhead lock is in place, however, this is not designed to solely hold the door closed. The rod designed to operate the warning light is good for just that. The door is closed, but not secured.

The air that causes enough low pressure over the top of the wing to allow flight also pulls the door opened.

Pushing with the palm of my hands, the door pops open. I also notice that when the door is fully open the bowed extension arms, due to lack of resistance at the doorframe, straighten out and fully extend the main locks. Even if I could get the door closed, Craig points out that it would only open again. I look at Craig and ask if this would have been found at an accident site. He replies, "I doubt it! But who knows?"

Later the secretary answers the phone at the FAA office and I identify myself and ask for Mark. During our conversation, he shows great interest and amazement at how far the door trailed open.

"What happened when you lowered the flaps?"

"I didn't."

There was a moment of silence before I speak again, "Mark, you might want to take a look at this one for yourself." He arrives about an hour later with a maintenance inspector. They both climb inside the airplane and see the problem firsthand. During our discussion I ask if there was new information about the accident he mentioned during our check ride. There was not. We discuss many ideas until finally I ask if there is going to be an incident report or an AD that might help, something to give others a heads up. Since this incident ended without a mishap or emergency, there is nothing to warrant any kind of formal acknowledgement from the FAA. I keep arguing that we have a machine in one piece and a possible idea of what could have caused an accident.

According to officials there is no concrete evidence that the door opening as it did could destroy enough aerodynamics to cause an accident.

My reply is, "Why are we looking at the door as the chief cause?" I point out, "In the aircraft flight manual, the only reference to an unexpected door opening is to close it. I do not think an aircraft would be certified if anything dangerous existed because of a door opening."

There is some agreement with that statement.

"Look at this band aid on my head!" Now everyone looks at me strangely."

"When the curtain became dislodged, I was temporarily incapacitated. This might have happened to the other pilot. He was on the later part of his approach; I was on take-off. That could be the reason I am here talking to you and the other pilot is not."

The airplane is repaired and returned to service, with the exception of the curtain, which remains in my office. A few days later I have a discussion with a friend of mine who also flies the same type of aircraft and explain to him the circumstances, "I pulled those things out the day the airplane arrived. Now I have two titles, chief pilot and interior decorator!"

Mark and a few others do unofficially acknowledge my statements but that is as far as it goes. Unofficially, the official word remains unofficial. (35)

E. A. Chevrette, Jr.

Chapter Thirteen

The Perfect Gentleman

While in the process of changing some revisions in the emergency procedures in the flight manual for the Piper Arrow, one of our instructors enters my office. Chris Mallory whose very energetic personality is expressed during conversation, coupled with his sense of humor, these traits are surpassed only by his sense of timing to engage in such activities.

"I hope that is a cookbook you have in your hand!"

Smiling, I reply, "Why?'

"After that last airport sponsored cook-out, everyone hopes you might take the hint. Those burgers were terrible!"

"I cooked the sausages remember?" I reply.

"How could anyone forget?" We both laugh as we pour ourselves some coffee.

Our conversation soon changes and centers on the revisions for the emergency procedures and their execution; Chris's serious side becomes apparent as he makes the comment, "I would certainly like to know who decided the previous emergency procedure needed revising." Our conversation ends in agreement; regardless of how carefully the procedures are written, there is no understanding of what it's really like until it happens.

Later that day as I thought about our conversation, I remember three specific flights that are more than noteworthy. I have had the opportunity to see human reactions under actual conditions; enthusiasm, false heroism and even panic. The situations range from only a few people directly involved with the incident that for the most part went unnoticed, to a whole township getting in on the act. One incident involves so many people, including the authorities that except for the people directly involved, resulted in much confusion. As with all, it is rare that the true story ever gets known to the populous, and the true identities of those shaping the outcome are rarely acknowledged.

The winds are light out of the north as we start our take-off in a Cherokee 140. Mike, one of my ROTC students, handles the take off well and quickly transitions to climb configuration. Once over the trees on the north end, our rate of climb parallels the rooftops of homes located on the hill just north of the runway. It is the last day of October, a beautiful day to celebrate Halloween and a great day for flying.

Just before we cross the top of the hill, I notice a slight hesitation in our power plant. I immediately apply carburetor heat. With no results, I reach for the ignition key; if there is a fouled plug at least I can isolate it. As I place the key to the left magneto, the engine backfires and quits.

There is an unwritten rule in aviation; if a switch or control change produces undesired results, return said item to its original position. As I return the key to both mags, the engine begins to increase RPM, but shortly thereafter backfires and quits again. Switching the key back and forth to left and right mags, then both, then separately again, I am able to keep the engine running in spurts between backfiring. Simultaneously, I lower the nose to maintain speed as we pass the crest of the hill that lies to the north of the airport; the large farm that lies beyond the hill will afford me some room to maneuver.

During my daily flying I have observed a few likely areas that could be used for an emergency landing. I have even driven my convertible around to several locations to survey the possibilities from the ground; one of which lies north of the airport beyond the houses on the north side of the hill. There is a straight stretch of road just beyond the trees that divides two farms. Here there are two sharp curves, one on the north and one to the south, bracketed by a guardrail on the west side and a house on a small hill to the east.

My attempts to find a working mag that will restore power beyond the spontaneous power surges between backfiring are unsuccessful. I instruct Mike to slide his seat back, tighten his belt and place both hands in the instrument panel; he calmly complies. I begin to size up the possibility for using that stretch of road for a landing site. My thoughts are soon changed as a slow tractor-trailer negotiates one of the turns and is now occupying that very same stretch of road. I manage a turn to the left in an attempt to find a field, only to find it out of my reach. I continue making small left turns away from the houses and trees, neither of which seem appealing for a landing site.

During the power surges I am able to maintain 80 MPH, which is the normal climb speed, and then I convert this speed into as much altitude as possible. This is accomplished only to a slight degree as the airspeed drops off to 70 MPH as the backfiring returns. I then lower the nose and repeat the same performance. All this is being accomplished while I work feverishly changing from one mag to the other to quell the backfiring and get one more burst of power. At one point I feel that only the muscles in my body are providing the lift to keep this airplane flying.

All the possible fields I have contemplated are not as readily accessible to me as I once hoped. Fields are full of equipment and or people; stretches of roadway are tied up with traffic. At one point, during a burst of power I find myself changing the throttle position hoping for a little more RPM. Still making small turns and corrections I am able to get the airplane turned around and parallel to the runway close to the swamp.

I now find myself gauging an attempt at another left turn and take a shot at the runway. Sizing the situation, my altitude is a mere three hundred feet instead of the normal eight hundred. At least for the moment I am away from the houses; should I not make the runway, there is always the swamp. I am still flying from one power surge to the next.

I have worked my way into a position opposite the runway threshold. Executing a shallow bank I plan to make this one continuous turn to line up on the runway, making the best use of altitude and whatever power I can manage. Turning onto a very short final I still work to keep the engine firing, and being this close, I find myself working even harder. I have the runway just to the left of the nose when the engine backfires again; this time is not followed by a surge of power. I continue the approach as I sink to the tree line located to the west of the runway. The turn is completed just in time to execute a landing on the same runway we had departed from moments ago.

As the airplane rolls to a stop, I open the door and take a deep breath. Turning to Mike I break the verbal silence and question his well-being. He is wearing a huge grin. Removing the tow bar from the rear of the airplane I climb off the wing. I feel completely drained, but try not to express this when addressing my student, "Well Michael, welcome to your first, shall I say, unplanned landing? I hope this does not dampen your spirits any?"

He is still smiling," "That was cool, I can't wait!"

I am almost envious of his youthful enthusiasm as I shake my head and pat him on the back.

As we tow the airplane from the runway, Paul joins us. He is a tall man about thirty, with a quiet yet deliberate nature about him. He is one of my commercial students and has witnessed the whole scenario from start to finish, "Do you guys realize you disappeared behind that hill just north of the runway?"

I look up at the house to the north and reply, "Great!"

As we approach the apron Craig joins us. In his jest he looks at me, "Sounded kind of funny Ed; is this a trick or a treat?"

With a weak smile I hand him the tow bar.

In the office I proceed with the necessary logbook entries for Mike including the time sheet for the airplane, which is kept in a small three ring binder along with the key. The entire flight had taken .2 of an hour, or a very long twelve minutes.

I then join Craig, who has removed the cowling and the back of the right mag located on the backside of the engine. The distributor timing gear on the right magneto has about one third of its teeth missing, these are lying inside the mag casing. Removing the back of the left mag shows a similar condition, if not slightly worse. I can hardly believe my eyes.

Craig looks at me, "So much for redundancy."

Outside of four people, two in the airplane and two on the ground, no one has the slightest clue how close I had come to parking an airplane in someone's back yard. Two days later an AD note came in the mail from the FAA, as usual, explaining in detail what some of us already know.

It is a pleasant Sunday afternoon; John Goodman, a newly enrolled student in the commercial Pilot Program, is at the controls of the Arrow as we enter the practice area south of the airport. Some of the maneuvers require cycling the landing gear. During a maneuver while extending the gear, an inoperative gear down light has successfully captured our attention. The nose gear and right main gear have green lights; the left gear has the malfunction.

Although not part of today's curriculum, it is an appropriate opportunity to learn the systems of the airplane. I quickly reach behind the left seat and extract the airplane flight manual and hand it to John. I instruct him to open to the emergency gear extensions checklist, and then further explain that the green lights are interchangeable; the first step is change bulbs with an operative light. Shortly, the blown bulb theory is eliminated. Second, we must watch the results as the gear is recycled. Same results. While all this is happening, John is showing outward signs of nervousness, in fact more than I would expect from him.

The gear is operated by an electric motor; the main wheels are mechanically connected and actuate simultaneously. The nose gear operates separately. John's face has become rather pale, as I ask,

"John, are you ok?"

"Are we going to land this thing with the gear up?"

"Relax!" I explain again how the gear works and why I believe the problem to be a broken wire. In an effort to keep him busy, on the way back to the airport I give him a basic navigation problem to solve.

I call the airport and explain to Craig the situation with a request that he stand near the runway for a visual inspection of the gear as I pass overhead. On the first pass, I notice several people running toward the runway's edge. On the second pass, there are almost a dozen people. After a brief conversation with Craig, we agree on the broken wire theory, however, without confirmation, it remains a supposition.

Regardless of any decision, the fact remains that I still have to land the airplane; I advise Craig of my decision. While preparing for the landing, I look at the access road to the airport and notice it is full of fire trucks, an ambulance, police cars, and what appears to be half the population of Poestenkill. Someone had apparently called in an emergency alarm. When I see what is happening, my only thought is a disgusting "Oh no!"

It is at this point John becomes even more nervous, "Oh my God, what are we going to do?"

"Relax."

I decide to land with the gear extended, keeping in mind the broken wire theory. On the later part of the final approach, I unlock the door, pull the mixture to idle cutoff and prepare to land without the assistance of the engine. If the gear does fail, this should minimize the damage.

After touchdown, I start the engine and taxi to the mid-field hangar. As I climb off the wing, a County Sheriff's Deputy greets us. As he looks inside the airplane he exclaims, "Thank God you are alright." With that, John seems to be full of an abundance of courage as he explains what a heroic deed he has just performed, and how he single-handedly saved the ship. I am so disgusted with all the theatrics that I decide to walk back to the office.

While on my way back to the office, a bystander stops me to tell me all about the incident, "Man you should have seen what just happened, I bet you feel lucky you weren't in that thing. It was a catastrophe." Once in my office I close the door to get away from all the commotion, shortly afterward Craig joins me, "Hiding again?"

I smile as I ask him, " Who called for fire and rescue?" We both shrug our shoulders. There is a commotion outside in the waiting room, as Craig and I enter, several people are asking questions about the airplane that has just crashed. Both Craig and I laugh at the ridiculousness;

an hour later the broken wire is repaired, and the airplane returned to service.

April mornings are usually looked upon with great expectations of spring and good flying weather. However, the great northeast and Mother Nature periodically remind us that the calendar pinned on the wall is not as official as we would like it to be.

Our departure from Poestenkill leads us directly to Albany, via the airway to Utica. On board the Arrow is Jim Jensen, a commercial student, appropriate navigational charts, four hours of fuel, and myself as instructor.

After complying with radio frequency and transponder code changes, we are south of Schenectady enroute to our destination. Continuing westbound, I find myself observing the weather with more than a casual glance. Although we are given a favorable weather forecast, what I am witnessing is far from it. As we encounter precipitation, I check with Albany and Utica, both are reporting good weather.

Beginning as light rain, its intensity rapidly increases. Within a few moments, closer observation provides a startling picture; the precipitation on the windshield stops flowing shortly after impact. The outside temperature gauge reads a minus one degree, and the probe for the temperature gauge extruding through the windshield is collecting ice. The right wing now has a glossy sheen from the precipitation. We are flying in freezing rain. Normally a climb to a higher altitude will put us in warmer air, but where? Nothing we are encountering has been in the forecast.

I instruct Jim to execute a 180-degree turn and head for Schenectady. I activate the pitot heat, the alternate air intake for the engine and disengage the automatic gear override. (36) As Jim executes a right turn, the freezing rain has mixed with sleet. Upon completing the turn, we have accumulated ¼ inch of ice on an airplane that is not licensed or equipped to handle such conditions. Engaging frequencies for Albany and then Schenectady both have favorable reports. A few miles west of Schenectady I contact the tower for landing clearance. Shortly after contacting Schenectady we are given landing clearance.

In operations, I contact flight service on the landline and inform them of the conditions we have just encountered. Fortunately I know the briefer; otherwise my pilot report might have been considered bogus.

Over coffee, Jim and I overhear an instructor and his student planning a flight westbound to Syracuse. I interrupt them and suggest they wait for an update; many disbelieving faces look my way as I explain the circumstances. I finally recommend they look at my airplane.

As Jim and I accompany them across the ramp, I can see the water dripping from the wings, tail and fuselage of our airplane.

After inspecting the coating of ice on the Arrow, one instructor comments that icing is not even remotely indicated in the forecast. Jim, a man in is late twenties, with well-kept medium-length black hair and black horn-rimmed glasses, gives a scholarly appearance. Add in his quick wit and his reply is priceless, "There is now!"

Within moments, a few more pilots join us, all of whom have their own comments. By the end of our gabfest, Jim and I are accused of being bearers of bad tidings and spiritual outcasts; how could we be the only ones to depart with the sun and return the same day only to be covered with ice? Looking toward the west, the same weather that we had just left is now fast approaching. After a few more chuckles, we remove what ice has not melted and decide to return to home base.

We are third for departure as we taxi toward runway 15. The lead aircraft departs to the southeast, I hear a young female voice explain she is on her long solo cross-country flight to Rochester NH, and would like to activate her flight plan. While waiting in turn for take-off, the precipitation starts, first as ice pellets, then sleet. The aircraft immediately ahead of us has already started his take-off when the precipitation starts; he immediately aborts his take-off and requests clearance to the ramp. Before the day is through this action would prove to be the smartest move anyone could have made.

I am becoming increasingly concerned about the student who has departed on her cross-country flight. Upon my own take-off clearance, I inquire of the tower about her location; she has been handed off to Albany Departure Control. Shortly after take-off I am handed off to the same frequency; here I am informed she has been handed off to the frequency controlling the eastern portion of Albany's airspace.

Passing overhead Albany I am handed off to the eastern controller; it is here the precipitation becomes intermittent. I recognize the voice over my speaker; it is Morgan, a long time controller at Albany. Morgan informs me he is still waiting on a weather update, as for the Cherokee ahead of us; she has already been cleared from the frequency. I report Poestenkill in sight; Morgan clears me from Albany's frequency followed by a transponder code change.

As I contact our Unicom frequency, an uneasy feeling is prompting my common sense thinking; I am through the worst of the weather with home base in sight. All that is left to do is land, cancel the rest of today's schedule and all will be well. However, this uneasy feeling is not getting any better.

Without explanation, I change back to monitor Albany's frequency; here I find the answer to this uneasiness. Morgan is in radio contact with the student pilot in the Cherokee. She has encountered the freezing precipitation and contacted Albany for assistance. The problem is that her transponder is inoperable; her aircraft is now a primary target, making radar contact in this precipitation impossible, particularly if the target is a light plane.

She has performed a 180-degree turn in an effort to return to Albany and escape the weather; in the process a very nervous voice is describing some of the landmarks around her. I hear her describe a body of water with a highway running over one end. While I am trying to visualize her location, she informs Albany what radial of the VOR she is on. This is another clue to her location. Morgan, with great concern in his voice, repeats he does not have radar contact; she continues broadcasting landmarks to Morgan.

I reach forward for the throttle and advance it to cruise power setting, pointing to a northeasterly direction, "Jim, let's go, Tomahannock Reservoir."

I contact Albany informing Morgan of our location, heading and transponder code of 1200. Morgan replies, "Radar contact." With that I inform him that we are heading toward the reservoir. Just east of Bald Mountain we once again encounter freezing precipitation. A few moments later I make visual contact with our target, informing Albany. Morgan reconfirms radar contact then informs us of the not so favorable weather report: ice pellets, sleet, freezing drizzle, and surface temperature minus one-degree celsious. The entire area is the surprised host to an unpredictable meteorological nightmare.

I explain to Jim that I want to get as close to the other airplane as possible, but not too close to cause alarm or undue hazard. With that he laughs, "Undue hazard? Great, I can't wait to see this introduction."

I try my best to appreciate his humor as I announce our position. "There is a red Cherokee pulling up along your left side. Do you see me?"

The precipitation has reacquainted itself with increased intensity. I can hear the relief in her voice as she acknowledges our presence. I proceed to ask her questions regarding her status and that of her airplane; fuel on board, instrument readouts regarding the health of the engine, altimeter reading. I continue this until I have an idea of the condition of the aircraft, her knowledge of the airplane and the stage of her training; so far so good.

"I want you to apply full carburetor heat then tell

me how the engine reacts." To this she immediately complies.

Albany has diverted all other aircraft to another frequency and controller; it is Morgan, the young lady and I. I too perform all I can in my airplane to combat this silent, potentially lethal enemy. The problem with ice is you never know when it is going to end. Before I can give any more instructions, a voice over my speaker makes my blood run cold.

"I can't see, I can't see, what do I do?" The voice is shear panic.

Our windshields are opaque with ice making forward visibility impossible, while at the same time deteriorating the aerodynamics of each airplane. To the uninitiated, this is a devastating experience. I know Morgan had heard this, as did anyone else monitoring this frequency. I am not sitting next to her in the same airplane to demonstrate what to do and help calm her fears. I must not allow panic to take over.

I shout into the microphone, "Relax! Forget the windshield. Use your instruments and me as a back up for your attitude, dress off on me and do what I do, go where I go. Now calm down. Do you hear me?"

There is no reply. I keep my fingers crossed hoping I have not made the situation worse. The next few moments seem like an eternity, my heart is pounding as her reply comes with a much calmer voice, "Ok, ok what do I do next?"

I have a reprieve. After taking a deep breath, I instruct her to turn on the pitot heat (37).

"I don't know what you mean."

"There is a row of switches next to your master switch for fuel pump, pitot heat, rotating beacon and landing light. Locate them!"

"Ok, I think I know what you mean. Which one do I turn on?"

"Turn them all on!"

With that, I contact Morgan asking for a weather update and informing him the icing conditions are not getting any better. Even Morgan is unnerved by the radio transmissions between the two airplanes as is revealed by the falter in his voice. The weather is unchanged.

I have been Jim's instructor since his first lesson, although he has always maintained his composure, today must be his ultimate test. A moment of silence is broken by Jim's voice informing me of something I am too well aware of; pointing at the altimeter he comments, "Ed, we are losing altitude."

To this I have no reply, for the ice is taking its toll. I start going through my mind and question all I know about weather trends. Weather such as this must have multiple freezing layers, there has to be warm air, but where?

I reconcile our conditions and find myself looking around for a place to land other than the airport. I know that the chances are slim with one airplane but even slimmer with two. I am very doubtful we will make Albany. At this point, my leg muscles feel as though they are the only means by which both machines are still airborne.

I keep up the chatter between Jim, Morgan and our newly acquired friend to my right; this is done strictly for medicinal purposes. My best hope is to get as close to Albany as possible. I look at the outside temperature gauge, minus one, the same as the surface temperature. All I need is a change of one or two degrees and the ice will change its properties to a friendlier one. Perhaps this is asking too much.

My thoughts are broken as a nervous voice asks about our altitude loss and whether or not it is intentional, she asks, "How am I going to see to land my airplane."

"Let's take it one step at a time. We'll get to the airport first. Hang in there we will be alright!' I say this with as much conviction as I can gather. Jim looks at me with a silence that seems to question our sanity. I return his look and ask if anyone has a better idea; we both know the answer. I reach down to open the air vent near the floor for some cool air, feeling the perspiration under my arms. It is ironic because on the other side of that window is ice.

My radio contact with Albany is the first information the controllers have received concerning this unforecast weather; in turn they contact the tower, who contacts flight service who in turn is conversing with the weather bureau. All facilities are questioning where this weather has come from, and why there has been no warning. In other words, where do we point the finger and why? In the meantime, Morgan is witnessing firsthand the seriousness of the situation.

We continue for a seemingly long period of time, when approximately seven miles northeast of Albany what I have hoped for becomes a reality. The ice is starting to peel itself off the airplane, first the right wing, within seconds the left until finally the airplane is clean. Looking at the outside air temperature, I see it reads a plus one. I immediately call Morgan, inform him of the circumstances and ask for an update on the weather. Even though both the IFR room and the tower are located in the same building, they are completely unlike each other; the IFR room is windowless. Morgan must get his update via the tower.

"Cherokee 918; visibility four miles, light rain, surface wind 190 degrees at five, temperature plus two. Stay on this frequency report turning final for runway 19."

Both aircraft are now ice-free. I pick up the mic and acknowledge Morgan's transmission then direct the rest of the transmission toward our visitor, "How are we doing over there?" By the tone of her voice I detect one large smile. I explain I will line us up on runway 19, there execute a go-around and from that location she should land her airplane. I inform her that I will circle and land behind her.

I report a short final and execute a pass over runway 19. I notice a 727 on the taxiway to the west of the runway; I later learn he and several other airliners expressed concern over the unforecast icing conditions. On runway 28, holding just to the east of 19 is a Mooney, whose pilot had landed at Albany without the aid of his communications due to the loss of an antenna because of the icing conditions.

As I execute a left 180-degree turn to enter downwind for 19, I notice our friend has followed every move I made and is presently right behind me. There is no way she is go-

243

ing to lose me. I make a transmission for her to turn inside of my airplane and land on 19, which she proceeds to do. Jim and I land behind her and taxi to the ramp. There is a light rain falling as we shut down the airplanes.

Jim looks at me, "Sure glad this is all over."

"Don't count on it James, don't count on it."

Making our way to greet our guest, I make a comment to Jim about what a difference a couple of degrees can make.

Standing about 5'4", with dark wavy hair that shows some signs of a hurried grooming, wearing blue jeans and a white long-sleeve blouse, our young "Student Pilot" seems to be keeping her composure rather well.

I ask, "Are you all right?"

"Yes what do we do now?"

"Well, seeing as none of us have an umbrella, I suppose it would be a good idea to get out of the rain."

Jim, with his great sense of humor replies, "You sure are of full of 'em today aren't you."

Once inside the operations building I escort her to a phone to call her instructor, tell him where she is, that all is well and to brief him on what has happened.

There are many people waiting in the lounge as we enter and all eyes are on us. While she is on the telephone, I am informed that another student had been turned around and sent to better weather conditions because of what Jim and I encountered. Including the Mooney I saw on landing, there were three other airplanes that were able to escape tragedy due to what was going on northeast of Albany.

I have just lit a cigarette when the young lady exits the phone booth, and informs me that her instructor said it would be alright to continue her trip. I almost choke on my cigarette, "What? Did you explain to him what just happened? Never mind, get him on the phone!"

Unfortunately, even the weather bureau has not caught up with what has happened, and as of yet, no one has updated any forecasts, at least not east of Albany. It is difficult explaining on the phone to her instructor considering he has no way to verify my information. He then offers to fly to Albany in a single engine airplane.

"Listen to what I am saying!" I explain everything again.

Finally, it is decided that she should stay here until better arrangements could be made. Apparently the whole pilot lounge could hear me, for as I exited the phone booth I could hear a pin drop, because all eyes are on me. Shortly thereafter, the weather changes for the better as rapidly as it had arrived. Jim and I return to Poestenkill.

I enter an office full of people, all with a look of disbelief as to what had just happened. Many of them had monitored the entire event over the frequency we were on, either through a ground-based monitor or aircraft radio. One at a time and then collectively, each person approaches me, wanting to know the full details, while looking for individual attention. I soon realize that to answer is just a waste of time.

I motion to Jim to follow me into my office. During our brief conversation surrounding the day's events the phone rings. A reporter from some paper, who seems to know more about what happened than I do, wants to write a story about our experiences. As he rambles on about heroes and the like, I hold the receiver between my thumb and forefinger, strategically placing it over the cradle at an altitude of about two inches and then I release it. As we exit my office, once again I am confronted with a barrage of questions.

I sum up the day in three words, "enough is enough." With that I call it a day.

In the evening I drive to Albany hoping to rendezvous with Morgan. Pressing the button next to the locked door at the base of the control tower, I introduce myself into the microphone. The door is immediately opened by one of the controllers, "Ed come in."

Inside the IFR room, radar screens that resemble round televisions, housed underneath a console to my left are installed along the entire length of the room. Each screen reports the response from each target as it interrogates the aircraft within its reach. The green glow from each screen, along with its corresponding keyboard, provides most of the light for the room. Occupying the third position sits a balding man in his late thirties, who, as I enter the room, turns slightly in his chair and slowly removes the combination headset and microphone from his head. I recognize him from previous visits I made with the students in my ground school; this is Morgan, working second shift. As I approach, he slowly rises to meet me. We shake hands and for a moment not a word is spoken.

I speak first, "Don't tell me I was you first customer

this afternoon."

"Not my first, but definitely my most interesting."

With that, other controllers enter the conversation, "Hey man, no more days like that ok?"

"Nice work."

As the conversations continued, it is evident that short of someone declaring an emergency, the situation was handled with the same "reverence." It is apparent that Morgan and the others were as surprised at the outcome as I was. Morgan and I retire to the break room where he pours two coffees. Together we discuss the day's events and I thank him for his help; to this he refuses any credit.

Looking at me Morgan finishes our conversation, "Things were a bit dicey for a while."

I can only shake my head in agreement. Our meeting lasts about a half hour. As I leave the radar room, there is a silent mutual respect as everyone returns to their respective duties.

Three FAA inspectors greet me as I enter the FAA office the following morning. The information they have received, much to my disappointment, is entirely different from what had actually happened. This whole situation has been more chaotic than I realized, to the point that I almost get the impression that I had ordered the bad weather! The four of us sit around a conference table as I proceed to fill them in with the facts, shedding a much different light on the subject. Everyone wants to point an accusing finger, but no one is sure who to point it at. After about an hour, Jack Pendleton, an inspector I have known for several years, requests that I accompany him to his office. A man of quiet and sincere character looks at me and half- chidingly states that he did not know whether this was luck or skill. I had no answer.

"I don't believe that airplane of yours is licensed to fly into known icing conditions." In reality, my gesture is actually in violation of the regulations. I reply, "It isn't."

"What you did is commendable, let's hope you do not do that again."

I have reached the point where it is more than enough; I thank him and exit the room.

Later that day, I am informed of an article in the newspapers about the incident. In the evening, I drive to Troy in search of a newspaper. The old hardwood floors of the newsstand have an annoying creek as I walk over to the section where the newspapers are displayed. On the front page of the second section is a half-page story. It is easy to find; a picture of a control tower and a small plane flying overhead. I purchase the paper and while heading for my car I read about the controllers, fire officials, FAA and weathermen; how everyday these heroes risk their lives to save wayward aviators and how thankful we should be to have such great people doing these thankless jobs. I stop reading the article halfway through and started it again from the beginning trying to find some resemblance of what is written and what actually happened. Better than halfway through the article one paragraph mentions my name and as a wayward aviator, I should be given some of the credit.

As I approach my car I notice a trash container with a sign on it, "Help keep our city clean". With that, I deposit the newspaper within.

As I enter my car a thought occurs to me; I never properly introduced myself, nor did I ask the young lady her name. Then again, I guess one cannot expect a wayward aviator to be the perfect gentleman.

The incident has brought out the best and the worst in the Monday morning quarterbacks, be they official or otherwise. I never heard any more from the FAA, Flight Service Station or the weather bureau concerning this matter. I think everyone involved is just happy to get this all behind them, which probably is also true of the young lady since I never heard from her either. As for me, it is another memorable entry in my logbook.

E. A. Chevrette, Jr.

Chapter Fourteen

Fortune Shines a Light

Cross-country flying provides the opportunity to get away from the familiar practice areas, navigate over different territory and investigate other airports. Although most of the trips are in the Mohawk or Hudson River Valleys, we have two locations that combine a higher degree of pleasure and challenge. These are the islands of Martha's Vineyard and Nantucket, Massachusetts.

Our flights take us from the base of the Berkshire Mountains to the flatlands of the Connecticut River Valley and over its vast tobacco fields. These flights continue over Hyannis, where we stay near the coastline until in a position to fly the shortest distance over water to the first island. Both islands host good airports with operating control towers and radar available through Otis AFB, located on the shore of the mainland. Taxi service is always available, however, it is more enjoyable to rent a bicycle and travel to the nearest beach or restaurant. Either mode of transportation provides great scenery; some dress in old New England architecture, others in bathing suits.

Fog is a factor and must be carefully considered when flying in or out of these two airports. Approaching Nantucket, to witness a sea of fog sitting on the water just east of the island extending to the horizon is not uncommon; this eerie looking white carpet is approximately 900 feet thick. Once on the move it can devour the island in a matter of minutes, leaving the airport closed for hours at a time. Other days, the village will enjoy the bright sunshine only to find the airport shrouded in fog, and sometimes it is the other way around.

On sunny days, when fair weather clouds are predominant, shadows cast on the water can easily be mistaken for an island. This gives a new challenge to navigation, especially since Nantucket hosts the last island airport before crossing the Atlantic Ocean. However, cross-country flights are not limited to island hoping; some are more environmentally inclined.

Standing under a large brimmed ranger hat is Mr. Schaeffer, 5' 2", wearing a forestry uniform laden with medals and appropriate badges. Speaking in a high-pitched voice, he introduces me to the inner workings of the forestry department and aerial fire reporting over the route contracted to fly. The route includes Rensselaer, Washington and Columbia counties, normally takes about an hour to complete, and is continuously repeated throughout daylight hours.

Mr. Schaeffer explains the equipment his department has supplied for each flight. One battery operated radio, including headset and microphone, a rather archaic looking unit used for reporting to the command center located on BeeBee Hill, in Austerlitz, New York. Three position reports are required on each flight regardless of the fire activity; departing and arriving at home base and the southern point of the route, near Copake Lake, New York. County Highway maps and a clear plastic grid sheet are tools used for locating each fire geographically. Since aeronautical charts used for aerial navigation have a different scale than the highway maps, interpolation is a key requirement. Of course, no contract would be complete without a clipboard and log sheet.

Throughout his explanation, Mr. Schaefer occasionally glances down toward one of his badges in what seems to be an effort to draw my attention to his decorations. Ignoring them seems to disturb him somewhat, and makes keeping a straight face an effort. This however, becomes even more of an effort when he issues my call sign: Twelve Romeo.

My call sign seems to elevate several eyebrows around operations. As a result, the schedule references the fire patrol as Smokey the Bear.

My first day after departing Poestenkill, I call in my position and note the time on my sheet. The reply to my transmission follows; Twelve Romeo BeeBee Hill on! The screeching, gravelly voice in the headset sends a chill down my spine and a piercing pain into my ears. With every radio contact this scenario is repeated. On one flight, I actually place cotton in my ears in an attempt to ease the shock. This, however, is not always useful due to the unpredictability of our reception. Sometimes I would have to hold the headset tight to my ears to hear the faintest of sounds, another time, placing the headset on the seat next to me is too close.

On most flights, I am the only occupant of the airplane. I soon discover that when it comes time to locate and report a fire, there is another entity that requires considerable attention; turbulence. Spotting fires, juggling charts and flying the airplane become an interesting sport, particularly when the airplane moves in more than one direction simultaneously.

When the afternoons become hot and humid, cumulus clouds form, some maturing into thunderstorms. The haze on such days restricts visibility in all directions except straight down. During this process, the turbulence noticeably increases, followed by intermittent drops of rain with a final greeting by distant lightning. This is definitely a demonstration of territorial domain with the storm always the victor. Days such as these would limit our flights to the valley portion of the route. The clearer, dryer days are more lucrative for spotting fires, especially in the mountainous terrain of the route.

One afternoon I notice a fire tower near Austerlitz, New York depicted on my aeronautical chart. I decide to pay a visit. Overhead I notice the tower sits in a clearing with little nearby vegetation, thus allowing an unobstructed view of the countryside, and unfortunately, little chance of a fire incinerating the tower.

This location will also allow an aircraft to approach from the west almost unnoticed, which I did. Allowing enough airspace, I fly toward the tower on an easterly heading, slightly nose down to gain airspeed. When positioned at about eye level with the tower, I pull the nose up into the vertical, executing a vertical 180-degree turn returning to my previous altitude while heading in the opposite direction. I listen.

There is a pause and then the silence is broken with a higher than normal pitch, "Twelve Romeo BeeBee Hill is that you?"

I reply, "Good afternoon BeeBee Hill, Twelve Romeo reporting."

She replies, "If you say so Twelve Romeo."

The next trip I approach from a different direction, this time flashing the landing light while heading for the tower. This brings a transmission telling me she is waving at me. I return a likewise transmission to tell her I am doing the same. I always laugh when picturing her waving in the tower thinking I can actually see her.

During the course of the second season, we apprehend an arsonist, both in the air and on the ground. Before the end of the season, the arsonist is arrested and charged. One immediate result is that Mr. Schaeffer receives another badge and medal. Unless he can find a shirt with three sleeves, I have no idea where he is going to put them.

Operations such as fire patrol, flight instruction, charter flying, and even the introduction of new airplanes is readily publicized in magazines available to the public. The major General Aviation Manufacturers, however, are always looking for unique ways to present their wares to the public. The Ninety Nines, a national women's pilot organization, is hosting a seminar at the Turf Inn, Wolf Road in Albany, New York, thus providing one of those unique opportunities.

The manufactures have supplied nine airplanes by count. The idea is to get these airplanes into the parking lot of the motel for all to see. It is first suggested to land them on a highway that paralleled the motel and then taxi down the exit ramp into the parking lot. The idea, although exciting, is not well received by town officials. An alternative plan is necessary, which begins with flying the aircraft into Albany County Airport. The remaining part of the trip is quite unique: the wheels will never leave the ground. We will taxi the airplanes on the streets of Colonie to the motel.

All the aircraft are brand new; these include three Beechcrafts, two single, one twin, four Cessna's; including a twin, a single engine Cessna on amphibious floats, and of course two Pipers. I put one of my students in charge of the Tomahawk. Since I have tail dragger time, I will personally handle the Super Cub. (38)

At 4:00 am the next morning, a rather wide-awake and joyful crowd gather in the pilots waiting area at Albany. During our briefing, it is discovered that most of the pilots involved are not familiar with the streets of Colonie. I inform the pilot of the Cessna, (fully equipped with amphibious floats), of the underpass that we have to negotiate which might cause a problem. The pilot, Hank, is very thankful for my input.

All bases are covered; we have our permits, FAA, and Town of Colonie Police as escorts. We finish our quick briefing and head to our respective airplanes. I climb into the front seat of the Super Cub and perform the necessary steps necessary to start our trip. This is one stunt I have yet to perform in a Cub.

All aircraft contact ground control, located in the tower, for our taxi clearance from the parking area. Even the controller has a good time with this one. He delivers his clearance in the same manner as that of an official IFR clearance to another airport, "You are cleared to the Turf Inn, via the ramp, thence the airport road, to Watervliet Shaker Road, to Wolf Road, direct. Do not pass go, do not collect two hundred dollars."

All appreciate his humor. The first airplane to leave the parking area is the Cessna Amfib; I am dead last in the Super Cub.

As I leave the ramp and jockey into position to follow the road toward the traffic light, I look over the left corner of the nose to get a glimpse of our procession. The wings of each airplane easily outstretch the width of the two-lane road leading to the airport. Periodically, some of our escort people have to remove a no parking sign to clear the way for our wing tips. Normally, the trip to the Turf from the airport is approximately six minutes; this morning by airplane it is one hour. This adds new meaning to the old adage; " when time is to spare, go by air."

With one third of our journey behind us, we shut down the engines and wait for help from our ground crews as we start negotiating light poles. I open the doors located on the right side of the Cub. On the adjoining road that leads to the nursing home is a parked tractor-trailer the police have stopped to allow the procession to continue. The driver climbs down from the cab and starts walking toward the procession. As he approaches my airplane, he hands me a legal pad and pen, "Here!"

Of course I look at him as though he is joking, "What's this?' I ask.

"I need your name and address." With that, I decide to have a little fun.

"You mean you want my autograph?"

"Not exactly, you see my boss is never going to believe me when I tell him why I am an hour late." I cannot let this moment pass without enjoying every second, "I know what you mean, especially at this hour of the morning."

With that, we both smile as I ask for his name and write the note:

Dear Boss, Please excuse your driver, Ralph, for being tardy. He has taken a wrong turn approaching the airport, causing him to arrive on the runway, whereby he has stopped and asked me for directions. Signed, Ed.

A few minutes later, we start up and continue toward our destination.

We approach the Northway Bridge, Rte 87, just prior to Wolf Road. The Cessna with Amphibious Floats sit high off the ground; add the arc of the propeller and the vertical tail and it is a very tight fit. All engines shut down again, with virtually only inches to spare, and several pilots engage in very carefully wing-walking the Cessna under the bridge. In the meantime, our procession is at a standstill.

There is now enough sunlight, making objects easier to see. Through the open doors on the Cub, I can see what appears to be a person walking down a driveway approaching my airplane. A pair of fuzzy bedroom slippers peer out from under a long robe. Continuing my assessment I notice a curler that seems to be out of place and hanging down to one side. This person is making her way to the mailbox, the one that is now directly underneath the right wing of my parked Super Cub.

The woman crouches under the wing of the Cub and extracts her morning newspaper. This I feel deserves comment, "How's that for service? Your paper arrived air mail this morning."

I think this to be quite original in content. She proceeds to express her disdain for airplanes and people who dare think they have a sense of humor at this hour of the morning.

Pointing in the direction of the airport she says, "Besides young man, the airport is that way." With that, I close the doors to the airplane.

Once again, we are underway. Approaching Wolf Road, the procession turns right while the early morning traffic starts to gather behind the barricades. One woman obviously shocked to see airplanes on the road in front of her, sits in her car and stares straight ahead. Next to her, one man actually gets out of his car and starts yelling, "way to go." The next motorist just buries his head in his arms and waits. Continuing down Wolf Road, I am surprised by how many people are gathering, many with cameras, to see this parade of airplanes. As we all taxi into the parking lot, some of the airline crews leaving the hotel for their early morning flights join in the excitement.

During breakfast, the discussions are lively. Hank approaches me to exclaim that his airplane actually fits under the bridge. The pilot of the Beechcraft Dutchess had brushed the bushes with his right wing alongside the roadway. When questioned about his intentions while in the bushes with the Duchess, the entire room breaks into laughter. Of course, I am not left out. I am questioned about my conversation with the woman retrieving her paper; it seems she called the police to complain about a lost airplane that was blocking her driveway.

During the two-day display, curious seekers and aviators alike arrive to participate in this unusually located display. Our Parade made headlines and TV news as far away as Germany.

The remainder of the summer and fall are busy; the onset of winter brings shorter days and the seasonal end to our trips to the islands of Massachusetts. On this particular winter afternoon, we are enjoying a cup of coffee as we prepare for a return trip from Westfield Massachusetts.

Departing on a northwesterly heading, with the cold front behind us, the weather ahead looks very promising. Although the cabin heater of the Cherokee 140 is working well, I am looking forward to getting home and relaxing by a cozy fire. Our flight plan should have us arriving at Poestenkill just around dark. Onboard is Doug Coleman, my student and his brother Joe who is occupying the rear seat.

We are engaged in conversation comparing the amount of snow in these hills to that at home in the Hudson Valley. I notice a large snow shower just to the west of Pittsfield, and judging by its speed and intensity, Pittsfield will soon become IFR. I turn to Doug, "Let's top it, go for 8,500 feet."

Doug complies, however, his brother in the back seat looks a little nervous when I mention the altitude, and he begins asking questions. I inform him that this is a common procedure to follow in this situation. The only disappointment I have with this flight, is that the winds aloft are considerably higher than forecasted and our ground speed is slower than planned. I will soon discover that the snow shower and winds are not the only unexpected conditions.

Approaching 8,250 feet, the instrument lights seem a little dim, so I reach over and adjust the rheostat that controls the intensity of the lights. There is no change. I then start a meticulous scan of the instrument panel; engine instruments normal, alternator light out. The VOR needle shows little signs of vitality as it lazily centers itself, and the on/off flag fluctuates. I turn up the volume for the VOR frequency; the Morse code identifier for Albany is very weak. Doug turns to me, "What's wrong?"

"I think we are losing our electrical system." I check our outside conditions and notice that we are on top and the sun has now retired for the day.

Doug is doing his best to reassure his brother that all is ok as I turn the navigation portion of the radio off to save power and proceed to contact Albany Approach Control. Although we are not transponder equipped, he might be able to get a primary target on us. I report my estimated location and altitude along with a brief explanation of our predicament. I receive a faint reply from Albany, "Negative radar contact, be advised, special weather observation, Albany is 2,000 overcast and two miles in snow." Under normal circumstances, an instrument approach to Albany would be academic.

I contact Poestenkill on the flight school frequency. Knowing the radio is getting weaker; I speak in a much louder voice into the microphone. After turning up the volume control, there is a weak reply from the ground, "The runway lights are intermittent, we think we have a short..." I lose the rest of the transmission. Realizing I will have little or no assistance from the ground, I set about trying to find a solution using only what we have, "Doug, hold this altitude and heading." In my mind, I am visualizing the electrical system; the rotating beacon is all that can be spared to conserve power.

I look at the master switch. It is actually a split switch, red and tan in color. This switch can activate both the battery and the alternator simultaneously or independently. My next thought is a malfunctioning voltage regulator. If this is the case, I can briefly remove the alternator from the circuit then turn it back on. This might jar the regulator and possibly restore my electrical system. It is worth the try.

I reach over to the alternator switch and place it in the off position, I wait for a brief moment; no difference. This leads me to believe I am on the right track. With that, I return the switch to the on position; the response is immediate and quite unexpected.

A blinding waterfall of sparks flies out from underneath the instrument panel. Coupled with the acoustics of loud crackling sounds, our first reaction is to cover our faces and protect ourselves, however, this is not going to stop this frightening pyrotechnic display. Covering my face I place the alternator switch back to the off position, this alone does not stop the fireworks; it is necessary to turn both alternator and battery switches to the off position, thus rendering our electrical system inoperable. We are now in total darkness.

I fumble around to find the pouch near my right ankle for a flashlight; which proves as useless as our electrical system. I now detect an odor, which could be the residue from our pyrotechnics or a resulting fire. Either way, my concern for fire is making me very uneasy. At this point, I glance outside only to witness another problem.

"Doug! Do you have any cigarettes?" I ask

"Yeah!"

"Light up a couple, quick!" I respond abruptly.

We have been so preoccupied with our fireworks display that we have inadvertently flown into the clouds.

We are both puffing on cigarettes to keep the tips as bright as possible and with hands steadier than should be, we alternately hold the cigarettes up to different instruments to monitor the aircraft's performance while we try to climb out of the clouds. Within a few moments, we are back on top again.

My mind is working as fast as my heart is beating. I have no communication capability. The directional gyro is set using the magnetic compass, my only source of navigation, and considering our electrical problem its reliability is in question (39). Returning to Pittsfield is not my best choice. Night flying, single engine over the mountains under good conditions is not one of my favorite sports; add to that the possibility of dealing with heavy snow showers and this is not enticing. Albany is out of the question. Entering controlled airspace under these circumstances unknown to ATC and other traffic is pure suicide.

We have plenty of fuel on board, permitting a flight north to Glens Falls or south to Columbia County, the latter sounding more realistic. Either direction, I will be crossing heavily used IFR air space and risk the chance of collision. The inability of accessing weather conditions for either location makes any decision highly speculative. If we break out of the clouds, ground contact will help with the solution. The odor is still with us and the possibility of fire is still on my mind as my uneasiness continues.

I inquire of Doug and our passenger, "How are you guys doing? Still with me?"

From the back seat came an unexpected remark from our nervous passenger, "Where did you expect me to be?" I consider his attempt at humor very courageous.

Doug inquires of our next move.... I reply, "I am still thinking that one over."

As Doug fumbles to light another cigarette from the last one I ask, "How are the cigarettes holding out?"

"Almost half a pack left!"

We could be close to Poestenkill; however, the cloud cover and lack of runway lights proves useless. I start searching farther beyond the airplane for something familiar, when suddenly there is a break in the clouds, below I see some lights. There are a few more wisps of clouds and then a small cluster of lights below us. Looking to the right, in total disbelief, I can see the runway lights at Poestenkill. Under normal circumstances, I would give this hole in the clouds a passing glance, without the slightest thought of actual engagement. Tonight requires a different approach.

I give Doug my cigarette, "Call out the altitudes!"

In one motion I throttle to idle, carb heat on full, rolling into a step right bank, I start spiraling toward the lights. This is a one in a thousand chance; my nerves are definitely working overtime.

Doug's voice is the only one heard, "Eight thousand. Seven-point five. Seven thousand...."

Every few seconds, it is necessary to advance the throttle slightly to clear the engine; it is also necessary to clear our ear passages due to the rapid loss of altitude. The tightness of the turn required to stay within the geographic boundaries of this hole in the clouds produces extra g loading on the airplane. This gradually diminishes as the opening in the cloud enlarges during our descent. After several turns, my reference point disappears, the runway lights go out.

"Damn."

I recover from the spiral when the altimeter reads two thousand feet. Without Albany's altimeter setting, I dare not go lower. With a few scattered streetlights and the help of Doug's cigarette for orientation, I pick up a westerly heading. Looking over the nose, I can see more lights; some in the background look fuzzy indicating approaching snow showers. I can feel my heart pounding, and the perspiration running down my side under my shirt; I must keep some composure. Looking over the right wing of the airplane, I catch a glimpse of the runway lights flashing on, off, then on again.

"Doug! The lights!"

My only hope is that they stay on for just a few more

minutes. I execute an immediate right turn; then full right aileron, left full rudder, throttle closed. I proceed to slip the airplane as much as possible to lose altitude. For an airplane not noted for good slipping capabilities, I am doing my best to change that. At one point, I think my left foot will protrude through the firewall while counteracting the displacement of opposite aileron.

I have but one shot at the runway. Applying full flap changes the sound of the air passing the fuselage. Gauging by the rumble, I am sure I have lowered the flaps at a higher than normal airspeed. All eyes are on the approaching runway lights. We all have one common thought; how long will the lights stay on? I continue the slip until the aircraft approaches the gravel bank that slopes to the threshold of runway 36. At this point I recover and execute a landing.

The midfield taxiway puts us in position to look through the window of the shop to witness figures darting in and out of the utility room where the main electric panel is located. One figure stops, and with surprised animation starts pointing out the window while making sounds audible only to those sharing the building. Some very relieved people approach me as I exit the airplane, and a very interesting conversation takes place.

Several people on the ground had monitored my transmissions with Albany and Poestenkill on a portable receiver, including the brother of my student and their wives. Gary, a part time instructor, had been engaged in conversation with Craig when I made contact on the flight school frequency. Before the evening is through, they are all involved with the ground-based electrical problems and work feverishly to restore power to the runway lights. The first attempts produce intermittent results, but their final attempt is obvious.

As the conversation continues, Craig opens the cowling, "Pew, something burned."

I proceed with a brief explanation of the evening's events for Craig's benefit when Doug calls my attention to the runway lights. Without explanation, they are again out of service.

As we walk back to the office, there is a barrage of questions, none of which I care to answer. Wearily, I open my desk and withdraw a cigarette pack while gathering my thoughts. This is the only lighted runway between Pittsfield and Albany, and both locations are IFR due to snow, which was not in the forecast. At just the right moment there was one hole in the clouds, which for the most part no one of sound mind would have chosen to enter. Add to this electrical problems with the runway lights, yet they remained on precisely for the duration of the landing. As I extinguish the match, I hear the voice of one of the wives in the hallway, "You guys got here just in time, it's snowing like crazy!"

Tonight fortune has favored the foolish.

The next morning I visit Craig in the shop. I am presented with one burned alternator, matching voltage regulator and one well-done battery. The positive post on the alternator had failed. When reengaging the alternator to the system, the surge of electricity was so great the components were burned out and actually blew the filament out of the two wing tip lights. This popped several circuit breakers, and arced through some wiring. Even the magnetic compass needed recalibration. The radio was unaffected because I had turned it off. It was only a forty-five minute flight from Westfield; the last fifteen minutes seemed an eternity.

Spring weather arrives, and with it, Twelve Romeo takes to the skies for the third season. Returning northbound near the Columbia County Airport, the skies are clear and the air smooth. Today's flight is completely uneventful; looking northward along the beautiful Hudson Valley, I relish the warmth of the sun as it penetrates the Plexiglas windshield. I would like nothing better than to curl up and take a nap, which I think is quite appropriate for this moment, for I have just flown my 10,000th hour.

Throughout this spring, as with others, my schedule includes many new students. On this particular morning, the wind and weather are ideal for a first solo, as is my student. We are forty minutes into the lesson, flying a new Tomahawk. After the next landing, I perform my usual ritual; casually turning to the student, I will ask how he would like to try one himself. I have done these countless times before; I expect nothing out of the ordinary except a good performance.

The airplane crosses the threshold of the runway and proceeds to a perfect transition for a landing. Something has caught my eye. As I glance at the left wing, I am startled by the sight of a deer running out of the swamp and toward the airplane.

I take over the controls to initiate a go around, but

just as I open the throttle, the animal runs just ahead of the leading edge of the wing. We are very vulnerable; the aircraft is just above a stall, close to the ground and the power has not taken full effect.

As the aircraft accelerates the deer turns left to escape the airplane, as he does the left wing makes contact and rides up and over the animal's back. The deer is pushing up against the wing and I am concerned the animal might turn toward the right and try to escape under the landing gear or into the propeller, which will result in certain disaster. I immediately apply left aileron to hold that wing down on top of the deer and opposite rudder to keep the machine straight. The wing actually rides up and over the back of the deer, causing him to tumble head first toward the runway. Concerned the hooves will cut into the skin of the airplane I proceed to fly the airplane a short distance down the runway. The deer is just getting to his feet as I turn the airplane around on the runway to survey the situation. After one look at the airplane, the deer disappears into the woods.

That afternoon, Craig inspects the airplane and although the damages are minimal, $178.00, the airplane is grounded.

I call the FAA office to report the incident and inquire about any required forms I might have to file. According to Mr. Gerald James, lead inspector, there were two other deer incidents in Albany's jurisdiction in the past forty-five days. Both aircraft sustained considerable damaged. During our discussion, he shows little signs of concern as he inquires about the disposition of the deer. We both laugh as I told him the deer got away. Considering that the situation was completely uncontrollable, and I have never damaged an airplane previously, he does not pursue any incident report. I thanked him for his consideration.

Chapter Fifteen

A Formal Challenge

I have been engrossed in this operations manual for nearly an hour. The highlighted information and dog-eared corners of each page are evidence I am not a stranger to its contents. Mark Mahoney and I co-wrote this manual for our charter operations. We are listed as Director of Operations and Chief Pilot, respectively.

The airport at Ogdensburg, New York offers little in the form of entertainment; reading helps pass the time while waiting for our passengers to return to the airport. Closing the cover, I place the operations manual on my lap and reminisce about the day when I first opened the flight manual of a very interesting aircraft.

Although possessing an Airline Transport Pilot Rating, I am once again enthusiastically studying in preparation for my new assignment, one that comes with a faster lifestyle, more complex systems and a very sophisticated office; one Learjet 24F.

Mark Mahoney and I are sitting in the pilot's briefing area. Over coffee we are discussing the day's flight, which will take us to Tallahassee and Tampa. Mark is pilot and instructor with the company that owns the Lear and a Turbo Commander 690B. His straight black hair, round face and smile are complimented by a firm handshake. He is very people orientated and perceptive; coupled with his military background, you have an instructor who knows how to get his point across.

At the north end of the ramp sits the white Learjet with its two full-length blue and yellow accent stripes on either side of the fuselage. The pointed nose and "T" tail give an impression of speed even while sitting on the ramp. There is a very provocative look about the airplane as the late morning sun reflects off the wing tip tank and stainless steel leading edges of the wing and tail.

Opening the split cabin door exposes one to the smell of the earth tone leather interior. The two carpeted steps in the bottom half of the access door and the cabin center isle is covered with a protective leather walkway. To the left the bulkhead supports a built-in bar and coffee container.

The passenger compartment houses two overstuffed, reclining, swivel leather chairs that match the forward facing leather bench seat, two folding desks on either side of the cabin and an in-flight phone to provide the passengers with a traveling office. The comfort of the seats more than compensates for the relatively small passenger compartment.

The front office has an instrument panel recessed underneath a shield to protect it from glare during flight operations and includes an annunciator panel with all the warning lights for each of the aircraft's systems. The flight director system, located in front of both pilots, includes all communications and navigational equipment including an off-course computer that allows me to electronically move any radio station any place I desire for navigation. The actual control console for this system is about the size of an eyeglass case.

Engine monitoring instruments are located in the center of the instrument panel, while the cabin environmental controls are located in front of the co-pilot. There are countless circuit breakers located on both sides of the cockpit and behind each pilot, some requiring monitoring by the pilot in the opposite seat.

Behind the thrust levers is the latest airborne radar. This reflects both weather and ground clutter, which will show up in color and intensity on the screen. Mark firmly points out that bright red signifies either a thunderstorm or a mountain; both of which should be avoided.

Preflight preparation of the aircraft requires two man-hours, including filing of the flight plan and load manifest. Operational hourly cost of $1,000 is considered normal for this airplane, with maintenance being the larger portion. To drive home his point on maintenance, Mark shows me a copy of the repair bill to replace the stainless steel, anti locking disc brakes for the main landing gear; the cost for repairs is $3,000 per side.

"Use them judiciously."

Most civilian transport aircraft of this day cannot cruise much higher than 35,000 feet; cruise altitude in a Lear is 41,000 feet, and frequently we fly at 43,000 feet.

One incident that requires my getting used to, is when the bulkhead behind the pilot's heads, when expanding due to the pressurization, makes a loud crack as we pass 39,000 feet.

Upon reaching reach 43,000 feet, Mark disengages the autopilot and allows me to hand fly the airplane. Human nature has me comparing this machine to those

I have previously flown: I am now 40,000 feet higher today than I was on my first flight in the Cub. Power is supplied by two engines, each rated at 2,950 pounds of thrust, as opposed to one four cylinder 65 horse power engine. Economy cruise airspeed is Mach .77, rather than 75 mph. Cabin pressurization altitude is 6,600 feet; more than twice the altitude I flew the Cub. The total fuel on board at take-off is greater than the gross weight of the Aztec. Fuel consumption is 1,200 pounds per hour; this is equal to the total weight of the Cub. One item is without comparison; the outside air temperature gauge indicates a chilling 60 degrees below zero on the Celsius scale.

I look down on top of weather that would normally hold me captive for hours until I reach my destination. Glancing at the horizon as we progress away from the warm front we have just flown over, I can actually begin to see the curvature of the earth. The one thing, however, that has not changed is the smile on my face. I remove my coffee cup from its holder and sip the contents in toast of this event.

New terms and emergency procedures are learned and practiced without variation; three prove quite interesting. The first is interpreting system failure alarms, fire warning lights, and extinguishing equipment. The second; emergency descents in the event of an explosive decompression of the aircraft cabin. The third is the loss of an engine on take-off after passing the critical V1 speed. At this speed there is literally not enough room to stop the airplane on the runway, therefore, the airplane is accelerated to lift off and the remaining single engine procedure is accomplished once airborne. (40)

Fort Lauderdale Executive Airport is one of our more frequent destinations. The first half of our route is over land to Wilmington, North Carolina, where we fly over water as we transition to the Atlantic Route (AR-1) direct to our destination. Although our altitude will place us above most visible weather, it is not always accomplished without a price. When encountering the jet stream, we are faced with two problems; strong headwinds that consume time and fuel, and high altitude turbulence. The airspeed range between slow and high-speed stall is very narrow at high altitudes, thus a level flight attitude must be closely monitored.

On cloudless days I take a moment to enjoy the panoramic view of the east coast, or to catch a glimpse of the massive wingspan of a 747 below. Enroute, when encountering thunderstorms not too numerous to cause diversions or delays, I indulge myself and electronically dissect one on the screen of our airborne radar, comfortably knowing that the beast is contained and is a safe distance from the airplane.

Keenan, a blonde, athletic 23-year-old collegiate type, is actually one of the fixed-base operators at Fort Lauderdale. He and his crew are very cordial and always treat us more like friends than customers. Upon our early evening arrivals, he and his staff will join Mark and I as we travel by golf cart to the large restaurant located on the field adjacent to the outdoor air museum.

During any layovers, Keenan places our airplane inside the hangar next to his personal Learjet. There, to complete the picture, his family's three Rolls Royce automobiles flank both airplanes. Standing between the two airplanes, Keenan, Mark and I engage in conversation.

Keenan becomes very demonstrative while explaining in great detail his flying adventures to Mexico and Venezuela. No matter where he lands, the Lear attracts much attention, not only for its looks, but also for the amount of noise the airplane generates. Smiling sort of sheepishly, we all agree that Lear pilots enjoy a certain amount of satisfaction knowing we are making all that noise.

Keenan, while discussing the addition of more airplanes to his corporate and charter business, refers to his airplane as his wings of fortune. Before our conversation is through, he offers Mark and I, with our airplane, a position with his company. This allows Keenan versatility while at the same time it allows Mark and I the access to pertinent information and exposure in preparation of our own operations manual. Although temporary, Albany is now a satellite base for Keenan's operation. Within six months we will prepare for our own.

Millard Crane's voice is deep yet soft spoken. He is attractive and stylishly dressed. Although competent, he seems quite young to be an FAA inspector. His recommendation was instrumental to my acquiring this position with Mark.

During our meeting we joke about our first conversation that was held over a snow shovel. During his transfer to Albany, Millard had landed at Poestenkill shortly after a snowstorm, and while taxiing off the runway, his aircraft landing gear bogged down in a snow bank.

Before our conversation ends, initial papers will be filed and work begun for FAA approval. During the subsequent weeks that follow, Mark and I will produce our own operations manual and will proceed with the required proving flights. On an early warm summer afternoon, Mark, Millard and I prepare for the final check ride for our charter license approval. At the end of the day's flight, Millard gives his stamp of approval on our operations as well as my Learjet type rating.

The next afternoon while looking through the office picture window at the mezzanine overlooking both airplanes, a familiar figure approaches the stairway. It is Tom Lawrence, a former student and long time friend. After a generous handshake and a "how are you" our real conversation begins. His well-groomed blonde hair is usually complimented by his rosy complexion and a huge smile; today both are missing. I know something is wrong.

His voice brakes slightly as he speaks, "I know you are aware of the illness of both Lou Slatterly and Walt Grimm."

I nod my head in return. Lou Slatterly was long time operator of Round Lake airport and seaplane base. Walt Grimm, whom I had known since my early days as an instructor, had been one of the flight examiners for my graduating students. I am greatly sorrowed with the news of their passing. Later that day over a cold beer I inform Tom of the status of the new charter company; we end our meeting with a reflection on the past and a toast to the future.

A warm Sunday evening in July finds Mark and I preparing for yet another departure to Fort Lauderdale.

A strong cold front to the west is not expected to pose any problems to the flight, but it is still considered in the overall picture. Several local thunderstorms, not associated with this system, have developed near our destination and should be diminishing at the time of our arrival.

Approaching JFK at 41,000 feet, I close the aluminum flight log containing the pertinent information of the flight, and place it in the holder next to me. The eyebrow shield over the instrument panel prevents the intrusion of light from outside sources while reflecting the green glow of the instrument lights. I reach up to turn off the map light and reset my armrest. In doing so, I take a brief moment to relish the lights of the city from a chair that is seven miles above them.

Just south of JFK, we become audience to a show that has been produced, directed and choreographed by nature and is completely inaudible to this audience. To the west, a line of thunderstorms is putting on a display of pyrotechnics that whets the imagination. In an unleashed display of sheer beauty and unimaginable strength, each storm cell makes its contribution, which in turn triggers others to follow suit. Resembling a large x-ray photo, each storm's inner-working is exposed against the darkness of the surrounding sky as each marks its territory. At one point, the entire length of the cold front displays its beauty and might so fiercely, I can almost see the deafening sound of thunder.

Night visibility at altitude is unrestricted, and without other visual references for comparison I have no idea of my proximity to these storms. I check our own radar; within its 400-mile, 60-degree arc range I show nothing. Without looking, I pick up the microphone to call Center for an update on this activity. Center returns my call after their inquiry of controllers to the west; the cold front is over 400 miles west of our position and trailing 700 miles to the south. Acknowledging his transmission I return to my duties. Initially our passengers are not as intrigued with this display of activity as I am. A brief explanation produces satisfactory results as the display continues for nearly an hour.

Approaching our destination, the scattered storms have weakened as forecasted with only a gentle rain hitting the windshield as we park on the ramp at Fort Lauderdale. The reactions vary as each passenger deplanes, from total silence, to smiles and thank you's.

The return trip the following evening treats us to a setting sun in the west while a full moon replaces it overhead. Sitting in the copilot's seat, I can see the sun reflecting off the bottom half of the right wing tip tank, while the top half reflects the light of the moon. The reflections of the aircraft's rotating beacons on the wing provide the only movement for what seems to be a total suspension in time and space. As we cross onto the East Coast again, the night is so clear that we can name the cities on our route just by their shape. Approaching the Big Apple, I adjust the antenna on the radar and map out the streets of Manhattan on the radar screen.

Dallas-Fort Worth airport soon becomes another familiar destination. Departing from Fort Lauderdale, we join the Gulf Route airway over Sarasota. On early morning departures over the Gulf, we experience the turbulence caused by the rising sun as it heats up the atmosphere. As the sunrise slowly erases the stars from the sky, the early morning provides a clear, smooth ride. The picturesque scene is scattered with numerous oilrigs and ships, along with the contrasting color of the muddy Mississippi as it flows into the waters of the Gulf. Passing New Orleans, we then proceed overland to Dallas.

One summer afternoon flight over this same route proves a little more interesting. Over the water, the storms are building so fast that we are notified by Center after our flight reaches New Orleans that the Gulf Route will be closed for the day due to these conditions. To those near New Orleans, this probably means little; however, when one has yet to reach the mid-point over the Gulf, this announcement has a little more merit.

We have already started our diversions both visually and on radar. Passing 35,000 feet we virtually watch a cumulous cloud out-climb the airplane to such a height we have to crane our necks to see the top. I request flight level 430 as our final cruising altitude.

Passing New Orleans, we leave the activity behind us, only to encounter another cluster of thunderstorms that has developed east of Dallas. Although not as high or severe as those over the Gulf, they still must be reckoned with. We deviate to the north before starting our descent; there we engage the anvil or overhang of one of these storms. Descending through 41,000 feet the ride is surprisingly smooth. I glance at the windshield, and then at the wing, and focus on the outside air temperature that at this altitude is normally 60 degrees below zero Celsius, however today the temperature has climbed high enough to develop structural icing conditions, enough to warrant activating the anti-icing system on the airplane (41).

Upon each arrival at Dallas, the passengers step from the airplane onto a red carpet placed in front of the aircraft doors. A van or golf cart transports them to operations, while the linemen fuel and clean the airplane. Departing is similar in fashion.

The controllers are just as cordial on this particular hot humid day as we taxi off the ramp weighing 13,800 lbs; their expeditious handling of our flight allows us to attain our flight plan altitude of 41,000 feet and cruise at Mach .77, in thirteen minutes ten seconds.

A new customer, IBM and a new destination, Houston Texas, has made its way to our flight schedule. Our first of many flights departs Albany well after midnight and our passengers are in Houston waiting for a 6am departure to Albany.

As I walk into the Flight Service Station at Albany, the sky to the west is consumed with lightning. Entering the briefing room, I am greeted by Nancy, a short, stout woman whose high-pitched voice has little problem finding an open ear, "What are you doing here so early?"

With that, I explain my presence. "Aren't we the early bird?"

After a good laugh I receive an in-depth briefing that includes the cold front to the west. While filling out the flight plan form, the rain pounds the windows of the briefing room with such force that normal verbal communications are barely possible. Within a few moments there are several lightning strikes, one of which hits the antenna atop the briefing room, while two more render all the airport lights inoperable. In the complete darkness of the room I hear Nancy announce, "And that was not forecast."

The flight is delayed two hours.

After take-off, we are given a left turn for departure, when suddenly there is a thud from the nose of the airplane. Mark and I question the noise while checking the annunciator panel for any warning lights; the panel is clear. After a few moments, we conclude that the nose gear door must have been slow to retract, and proceed about our business.

A glance at the radar indicates some minor remnants of the storm still ahead; its encounter should be brief thus giving us little concern. Getting prepared to change radio frequency, we hit two sudden jolts pressing both of us against our belts and harnesses. Looking at the windshield, I find something else that is not forecasted; it is coated with ice. I turn on the light to check the leading edge of the wing only to find we have accumulated almost two inches of ice and it is still building.

This presents a problem; anti-ice is usually activated just prior to or shortly after the first signs of icing. With this amount of accumulation, unmelted chunks of ice leaving the wings and engine inlets can cause damage to the engines. Although turbines are great engines, their digestive systems are not conducive to swallowing chunks of anything. With crossed fingers, Mark activates the anti-icing system while I monitor the engine instruments. Fortunately all works well.

Within a few minutes we are clear of the remnants of the passing storm and continue our climb to 41,000 feet. As the night becomes day, the aviation community is coming alive as evidenced by the increase in early morning communications. I jokingly turn to Mark, accusing these faceless voices I hear of keeping banker's hours. Bright sunshine and a cloudless sky greet our arrival at Houston.

Prior to refueling, I monitor the lineman as he attaches the ground line from the fuel truck to the nose wheel of the airplane. As I start a walk around the airplane, I notice that centered on the nose cone are the remnants of a fairly large bird; legs and feet stuck to either side of the nose, along with a few feathers. This must have been the noise we heard departing Albany. I find myself asking; what are the chances of this happening just prior to flying into unknown icing condition? Either situation by itself could have proven hazardous, but to have both in one night is a little concerning.

This has been an interesting morning; one that comes with two reprieves. Both Mark and I realize how fortunate we have been. To lighten up the morning, I turn to Mark, " You don't suppose that bird got his briefing from Nancy this morning do you?" With that we both laugh.

The return trip home is without incident as are the many subsequent flights during the remainder of the summer, throughout the fall and into winter.

With its arrival, winter brings the cold starts that require assistance from ground power units, snow removal from airframes and of course landing on slippery runways. Lacking thrust reversers, the co-pilot usually keeps one hand near the drag chute handle. However, the airports we frequent during the winter are the larger municipal type with longer runways, making this a precautionary procedure.

This morning the center of the low-pressure area is centered over New York and Long Island sound, headed for Boston. Most flights whose destinations are within the effects of the weather system are cancelled. New York airports are closed, and heavy snow has already reached northward past Albany. Our weather briefing includes icing and turbulence at all altitudes; tops expected around 39,000 feet. Due to the lack of traffic, pilot reports are not available. Although offered, I show little interest in accumulation estimates; a Nor'easter can produce as much snow as it wants to.

I proceed to fill out an official flight plan form; this includes pertinent information regarding the airplane, requested route of flight, fuel, equipment, souls on board, pilot's name and lastly the destination. Today it is Fort Lauderdale.

This storm will challenge the major populous to a game of survival, as roads become slippery and hazardous, airports and schools close, and with everything publicized for all to see.

The flight plan form I have filled out is placed into the computer for final approval. This, in a way, is a formal declaration to challenge this storm; technology and experience affords me the capability, while opportunity ignites the desire. When this flight is successfully completed few will know; should by some outside chance it is not, few will understand. I place a folded copy of this flight plan in the breast pocket of my blazer.

Preflight of the airplane is accomplished while inside the hangar; the airplane is then towed onto the ramp. Although externally we are of casual nature, there is a slight anxious feeling knowing that every move Mark and I make must be planned and deliberately executed in order to safely accomplish this flight, for this is our profession.

From our performance charts, we recheck the numbers for the maximum power and the critical airspeeds for this take-off. The checklist is read in a monotone voice, almost a chant. As each line is complied with, the starting procedures are accomplished and the aircraft systems come alive. Our route clearances are received with little delay and are followed by a clearance to runway One. Approaching the runway, I hear the tower hold the snow removal equipment on an adjacent runway for our departure. We are cleared for take-off.

The runway has taken on its wintertime face. Runway lights display the difference between natural and man-made white. As the snow increases in intensity, the power is advanced for take-off.

Our limited sphere of visibility, and the brief appearance of the centerline runway lights visually add to the rapid acceleration. V1 speed is called out. At this speed, individual snowflakes take on the appearance of a white haze. Seconds later, at 122 knots airspeed, the command is given to rotate. After lift-off, deliberate, crisp commands are called out, rapidly executed, and repeated back for: the retraction of the gear and flaps, activation of the yaw dampener and heading mode for the flight director. We have entered a world where all movement is reported solely by the instruments.

A climbing left turn is initiated to intercept our departure heading; passing 3,000 feet airspeed is increased to 250 knots. Shortly thereafter, the anti-icing is activated. The left engine de-ice light activates itself on the annunciator panel indicating that the intake for the left engine is without ice protection. All eyes are on this light for what seem an eternity; a few flashes and the light is extinguished. Turbulence introduces itself with an occasional jolt confirming a portion of our weather briefing.

Passing 10,000 feet, airspeed is increased to 306 knots. The intensity and frequency of the turbulence increases throughout the climb. I feel its resulting presence in the inertia harness and seat belt as they restrict my movements to what is within arms length. The 18,000 feet checklist is complete. With each frequency change, center replies quickly with another altitude change, thus allowing us an uninterrupted climb toward our flight- planned altitude. Although it is a busy morning in our office, I take a very brief glimpse at the inner workings of this storm with clouds so thick that they hide the tip tanks from view, and an overwhelming darkness-requiring the instrument lights to be set on high in order to see the panel.

Passing 25,000 feet there is another frequency change and a clearance to 33,000 feet; frequent turbulence remains throughout our climb. Another brief check of the wing shows the precipitation melting on the leading edge of the wing and departing as liquid over the top. Although the flight is going well, I almost get the feeling of being toyed with as a large cat with a small mouse, for if a storm were to have a personality, I would call this one feisty. Another frequency change and we are cleared to our final cruise altitude.

The turbulence and clouds end abruptly; we have passed the top of the storm at 37,500 feet. I reach into my jacket pocket and extract my sunglasses as does Mark. Placing them on my head, I notice the flight plan has fallen out of my pocket onto my lap. As if it were a souvenir, I promptly place it back in my pocket.

The close proximity to the clouds reflects our speed, while a visual check of the airplane reveals less ice than had been predicted. Once level at 41,000 feet I report the tops of the clouds to New York Center; 37,500 feet, they promptly acknowledge. The DME reveals a much stronger headwind than predicted, which means an unplanned stop at Wilmington for fuel.

Our uneventful arrival at Fort Lauderdale is accompanied by a warm sun and a slight warm breeze; factors that can be appreciated by two tired pilots. As we enter operations, I remove the flight plan form from my pocket and place it in the wastebasket. It is history, as is the storm.

The flights unsuitable for the Lear are flown in the

Turbo Commander 690B. With the fuselage slung below the wings, occupants have a bird's eye view, especially during take-off and landings. Passengers are fascinated while watching the main landing gear as it turns 90 degrees before retracting into the rear portion of the engine nacelle.

The airplane's capabilities allow flight at 25,000 feet and 285 knots airspeed. With the reverse thrust from the propellers, its versatility allows landings on runways such as runway 15 at Linden, New Jersey, which is approximately 1,500 feet long. The Commander is as comfortable at altitude as it is in and out of a small airport. It is not long before I develop a fondness of this airplane.

Our frequent flights to New Jersey terminate at Newark, while good weather days find Mark and I flying into Linden, New Jersey. Here, we experience fewer delays and different flight conditions.

Linden is an old airport that the city has grown up around, and ironically, as the residents move closer, noise complaints increase. Several of these complaints are directed at the Commander, which produces more than its share of noise. Although most approaches into Linden require clearing a large factory on the approach end of the main runway 33, which is considerably longer and farther from the noise-sensitive neighbors, the problem still exists. Our destination this day is Linden, and we are entering the New York Terminal Control Area from the North West (42). Mark, in the copilot's seat, acknowledges to the controller our clearance to 7,000 feet and the transponder code change. The sky is clear. From our position northwest of Newark we can clearly see the New York skyline.

When two pilots fly together long enough, the actions and responses of each are almost anticipated. All systems in the airplane are operating normally, yet for some reason this afternoon I feel an uneasiness that has left me without explanation.

I re-adjust my combination headset and microphone while checking our altitude at exactly 7,000 feet. Mark changes the frequency on the number one radio and reports our altitude to the next controller. I continue my outside vigilance; Mark follows suit. Without explanation I have decided to disengage the autopilot; Mark turns toward me with an inquisitive look on his face. Shrugging my shoulders I smile; Mark does likewise.

In an instant, an object has crossed into our path from right to left and is now centered in the bottom half of my windshield. I am suddenly on a collision course with a single engine Cessna. With only a spilt second to react, I simultaneously roll the aircraft hard right and nose up, while holding my breath in anticipation of a collision... it has been avoided. My reactions have resulted in placing the Commander in such a nose high attitude that if continued, will stall the airplane. I immediately push forward and to the left on the control wheel followed by left rudder to regain control of the airplane. Only the seat belts and harnesses are keeping both of us in our seats.

As Mark instinctively reaches for the controls I call out to him, "I've got it!" As we regain level flight, I look to my left, and there is nothing. Mark inquires, "Where did that 172 go?"

"Mark- that was a Cessna 182!"

He replies, "You have to be pretty close to tell the difference."

"Yeah, too close."

"Did you see his numbers?"

"He had small numbers on the airplane, but I did get 5S as the last two." With that, Mark calls the controller and explains what happened. The controller replies he had a primary target, which he thought to be a flock of birds; there was no other aircraft cleared into the airspace near us. The entire scenario is over as fast as it had begun.

Pilots have been known to sneak through this airspace without clearance on good weather days, and without radio contact or a transponder code their identity is unknown. The resulting collision and wreckage would be the only way anyone could have acquired information regarding the Cessna. I look at Mark; our experience and conditioning allow both of us to dismiss fright rapidly, and under the circumstances we both know that even profanity is a waste of energy. We proceed in silence to Linden.

On many flights in the Commander, I enjoy the company of Eugene, our co-pilot. He is a large, jovial, round-faced man in his twenties, whose knowledge of the Commander is impressive. He is quick to produce accurate performance figures and weight and balance data for each flight. He also has the ability to apply his sense of humor quite appropriately to his job.

Due to the noise, the Commander makes an easy target for the linemen to attract our attention and direct us toward their facility for parking and the sale of fuel. During engine shut-down procedure, the propellers are placed into reverse, resulting in a considerable amount of air being pushed forward out of the aircraft. Jokingly, Eugene brings to my attention the fact that should a lineman position himself close enough to the airplane, I can blow the hat off his head and half way across the ramp. While watching the hand signals from each lineman, Eugene and I make bets as to how far I can blow his hat away from the airplane. The facial expressions on some of the line personnel have been known to highlight our day.

Another of Eugene's memorable smiles involves departing a small airport in southern New Jersey. The lone taxiway does not allow full access to the end of the runway. While sitting in the take-off position on the runway, I notice tall poplar trees at the departure end, and at least 100 feet of useable runway behind the airplane. There is only a chain link fence dividing the end of the runway and an adjacent highway.

I look out the left window and behind through the spinning propeller while Eugene does likewise on his side of the airplane. Placing the power levers into reverse, I back the airplane up onto the usable runway behind us. I can almost sense the look on the passengers' faces for I doubt they have ever witnessed such an act. Judging by the amount of cars stopping on the highway behind us, neither have they. We have left one small airport in New Jersey with something to talk about.

That evening at Albany, while stepping out of the airplane, I hear a familiar voice, "Boy that's a noisy airplane you got there." It is Fred, my instructor, whom I have not seen in almost a year. I take him on a tour of both airplanes and our facilities while we bring each other up to speed over a cup of coffee. A short time later, we are joined by one of Fred's students. After our introduction, I explain he has the best instructor; this I know from experience. Judging by the expression on Fred's face I know he is pleased.

Both men depart and walk across the ramp while Fred explains some of the maneuvers they will be practicing. Judging by Fred's demonstrative gestures I know exactly what kind of flight it is going to be. What I do not know, however is that this will be the last time I will see Fred. (43)

My reminiscing has been interrupted by reality; I hear my name annonced over the loud speaker at Ogdensburg. Mark is calling from our office in Albany. We have known for several months that the parent company that owns both airplanes has been placed into receivership. Their financial difficulties had begun before we started the charter division. Mark informs me that the banks have taken the airplanes and tomorrow will be our last official day. We have one more flight before the charter department is closed.

Late the next morning, departing Portland for Washington, Mark and I, flying the Commander, find ourselves navigating around unforecasted weather that has painted a self portrait on our radar screen. The result of this will greet our return later that day with three-foot snow banks outlining the runway.

Visiting the museum in Washington helps pass the time; we forget for a few moments our own predicament and gaze in amazement at some of the first machines our predecessors had flown, and what courage they displayed in doing so. In the center of the General Aviation room is one of the first Cubs built by Piper Aircraft. Hanging from the ceiling above is the first Learjet - a well deserved historical salute to those who fly.

After returning our passengers to Portland, we have a brief conversation with the operator, who by now has heard the news of our predicament. He immediately hands us both an application for employment with his company, "Here, you guys fill these apps now." This is done in a very demeaning and demanding voice, something Mark and I have heard many times before. Many aviation department managers seem to gain a certain amount of self-unimportance by displaying such actions toward pilots. Mark deposits his application in the wastebasket, I continue to converse with a very attractive female co-pilot while completely ignoring our assailant.

Less than an hour later, we are cruising at 16,000 feet heading for Albany. As I look to my right, Mark enters the appropriate hours and minutes of this flight in the logbook and closes the metal folder with a definite snap. Even the dim cockpit light cannot hide the tired expression on his face. The countless hours required to open and operate a turbo-jet and turbo-prop charter operation have met an untimely end due to outside forces beyond our control. We have worked and flown together long enough that verbal communications are unnecessary; there are no words that can explain or ease our disappointment. Throughout all the hours spent in the air, both of us have successfully played the hands we have been dealt. The question remains; When is enough, enough? and who makes the final call?

Mark places the logbook in the pouch adjacent to his right leg and turns off the overhead light. Looking ahead at a cloudless, star filled sky devoid of anything except a smooth serene ride, we share a common thought; this is a beautiful night for the last flight home.

Epilogue

One summer afternoon while visiting operations at Albany Airport, I come upon and old friend and pilot; Bill Wilkinson. He was a flight instructor at Loudon airport before I started taking lessons.

During our conversation, he informs me that the same company he has served as corporate pilot for most of his thirty year career, has decided to sell the airplane and close the flight department. At 58 years of age, he has spent most of his life aloft. Presently, the retirement age of most pilots is 60. With his career all but abolished, his only hope is that the airplane will not be sold before he retires.

I am looking at a pilot with more flying time than I, more experience in weather flying, a man who was teaching people to fly before I was old enough to solo. I wonder how many situations had occurred over the years where his decisions, judgment and skill were solely responsible for keeping someone else alive; even when it might not have even been known to that person. Today, all that is meaningless.

I listened to him for some time, trying my best not to show pity, which will not only embarrass myself, but also display a complete lack of respect. I purposely add little to the conversation since my news is not much better than his.

Leaving Bill at his airplane, I continue across the ramp and enter the FAA office to check on another old friend; Millard Krane. He was the FAA inspector who introduced me to the Learjet and eventually rode with me for my type rating. Much to my surprise, he has left the FAA and joined the airlines.

Leaving the FAA office, I realize that I must make a decision; disengage myself from aviation completely, or continue in my search. The latter having more appeal.

Time comes to pass and I find myself in the pilot's seat of a Cessna 421. A piston powered executive twin, although pressurized and well equipped, it lacks the speed and altitude capabilities of its turbine counterparts. This is the first twin-engine aircraft operated by this local company. Along with a previously purchased helicopter, both are reportedly for business use; however, most flights are personal in nature. I know it is only to be a matter of time before the same interest that made this airplane possible would also be its demise.

My main job is pilot and instructor to Eugene Kramer, owner of the business and both aircraft, and Tom Lawrence, a former student and long time personal friend, also employed by Kramer. These two men along with Millard Krane are similarly involved with another instructor on the helicopter.

This is the first official flight in the Cessna. Including myself, there are five souls on board; Eugene, Tom, Richard (our maintenance man) and Ron, another employee of the company. During our flight to Boca Rotan, each man will take his turn in the co-pilot's seat. There, he will get a chance to fly the airplane while I oversee their performance and explain the operation of the flight director.

On the last leg of the trip, the oil temperature gauge for the right engine displays a higher than normal reading. While performing my scan of the instrument panel, I can feel a sense of urgency in Tom's voice as he points to the gauge in question. My first step is to inquire if any of the other instruments are reporting a problem. The panel of experts, oil pressure, cylinder head temperature, exhaust gas temperature, manifold pressure and rpm all speak of normal operations, while in turn, unanimously pointing the finger of solution toward me.

Although this airplane is much more sophisticated than the Cub, it is still just a gauge. With that I remember a remedy; strategically tapping the gauge with one's index figure. The needle returns to its normal position and the problem is solved.

After our arrival, Tom and I secure the airplane for our four-day layover. I overhear Eugene discussing his aviation exploits with his constituents, to which I pay little attention. Crossing the ramp toward operations I happen to pass two people standing near a trainer and overhear some very familiar vocabulary regarding an upcoming flight. To this I give more than a curious glance in their direction. Once inside operations I lower my flight gear onto a seat near the window and take a minute to light a short narrow cigar; at least for the moment, my work is cut out for me.

Tom approaches me with a big smile on his face and pointing toward the trainer he informs me that, "The young kid is taking his first flying lesson."

I look out the window and for a moment I share the

wonder and enthusiasm expressed on the young man's face.

There are several trips and training flights in the 421 following our return to Schenectady. Enthusiasm for the Cessna is quite keen for several months, but as in most similar situations it wanes as fast as it begins, until what I had predicted becomes reality.

One evening I receive a call from Mark Mahoney. Millard Krane and Tom Lawrence were tragically lost in a helicopter accident in Massachusetts. This was not predicted.

Some time has passed, this evening, sitting in the comfort of my home, I ponder the numerous logbooks and cannot help but wonder; to what extent does an individual determine his own destiny? Maneuvers demonstrated on a flight check are recorded on a piece of paper in a deliberate order of their occurrence. Upon satisfactory completion, the applicant receives another form as proof of their success.

In the case of an accident or tragedy, another form is used and in graphic detail explains the probable cause, which is speculative in part, with words of impressive definitions that almost defy question.

We do not have a formal piece of paper that explains why one man can become the victim of his own deeds, while another walks away unscathed. All the planning, experience and knowledge can produce almost miraculous results one day, and yet in just one instance, can prove totally useless. In our debates we have described how his luck has run out, how fate has been unkind or fortune missed its mark. Yet by whatever name we choose, we dare not indulge in complete interrogation lest we become the object of much finger pointing or ridicule. Regardless of the reasons, the results are real.

Due to an unforeseen condition, temporarily I have become unable to pass the required flight physical. The decision to fly or not has been made for me.

Approaching the last entry in my logbook, I review the results of my own fortune. In toast, I sip the contents of a wine glass as I close the logbook for the last time.

E. A. Chevrette, Jr.

Endnotes

Chapter One

1. The access road was located on Route 9, just south of the Crescent Bridge.

2. Consists of one fixed dial. The face is calibrated in one hundred feet increments, and rotated behind the indicator.

3. Due to its lightweight, a sole occupant flew from the rear seat to maintain aircraft balance.

4. Bungee cords were nothing more than large rubber bands wrapped in a cloth type material. They were used quite successfully in light aircraft to absorb shock from the landing gear.

Chapter Two

5. The retrieval was almost as interesting as the event itself; after placing some old tires under the nose, three 50-foot ropes were tied to the tail wheel. Pulling each simultaneously at predetermined angles, the airplane was pivoted back over its nose and onto its wheels without additional damage.

6. This is a battery operated, portable radio, that is fastened to a small shelf near the ceiling of the Cub. This is used for navigating on the low frequency four course range station; adding a transmitting crystal, will afford limited access to control towers.

7. This was a knick name that fortunately did not stay too long.

8. The turn and slip indicator is a very basic gyroscopic instrument. The needle indicated the direction and rate of turn; controlled

by the aileron. The steel ball mounted in a liquid filled glass race, indicates a slipping or skidding turn; controlled by the rudder.

9. Two friends had departed a frozen lake in Renssealaer County with their ski equipped Aeronca Champ; similar configuration as the Cub. On board were two new brooms handles recently acquired through a relative who lived on the lake. Flying back to the local airport, they noticed one of the bungee cords on one ski had broken; leaving one ski tip pointed down. After a few purposeful passes at the local airport to gain attention, one pilot opened the window and held the ski in the landing position with one of the broom handles while the other executed a perfect landing in front of several excited onlookers. This incidentally, was done as an expression of their humor.

Chapter Three

10. A hand held, spring-loaded tool was used to punch a hole in the fabric. A color-coded indicator incorporated in the tool would reveal the fabrics integrity.

11. The fabric was Irish Linen, or Grade A Fabric, depending on the airplane.

12. Students are required on solo cross-country flights to get their logbooks signed at each destination. The man who signed my logbook was the owner and only instructor at Germantown Airport.

13. There is a factory built in handle near the tail just for this purpose.

Chapter Four

14. Communication and navigation frequencies were easily accessed accurately with crystal control radios. Each frequency number is easily read, and eliminated the necessity of fine-tuning with an adjustable control.

15. A series of incomplete loops and half rolls sequenced to appear as a figure eight lying on its side.

Chapter Five

16. Flying through the top of the haze layer slight turbulence is experienced passing into the warmer air above; once above the layer visibilities are greatly improved.

17. The beacon on top of the granite memorial can be seen blinking at night over seventy miles away

18. Due to the rapid sequential lighting, it is referred to as the rabbit.

19. A bank of 100 degrees, pitch of 60 degrees, or combination of either performed repetitively in rapid succession would cause the vacuum operated gyros to tumble and become temporarily unusable.

Chapter Six

20. There are some operators using banners for up to 60 characters that are usually rigged between two poles and snagged by a hook suspended from the aircraft as it flies between the poles.

Chapter Seven

21. During the season, the heaviest thunderstorms travel from Schenectady, New York, through the area between Loudon Airport and Saratoga, east bound toward Bennington, Vermont. Hence it's nickname, thunderstorm alley.

22. Whenever a situation occurs causing several incidents or accidents due to a mechanical malfunction, an airworthiness directive is issued.

23. It took two days and as many bulldozers to demolish the old hangar.

Chapter Eight

24. The aircraft engines are equipped with super chargers, sometimes referred to as turbo chargers.

25. This is known as minimum controllable speed, and can be affected by altitude, temperature and weight. In light twin-engine aircraft it is commonly referred to as Vmc (Velocity minimum controllable).

26. A similar incident occurred to an Aztec out of Glens Falls. Fuel vents for all four tanks were obstructed; the pilot feathered both engines and landed dead stick in a snow-covered field, gear up. The aircraft was towed to a nearby road, where, with the aid of jacks, the landing gear was lowered. The fuel vents cleared and the airplane was flown back to its home base.

Chapter Nine

27. We have prepared flight plans just for the Milwaukee flights with built in headwinds for both directions. Set up as a scorecard, the time elapsed at each checkpoint is referenced by a plus or minus minutes in the air. This information is used for the decision to fly the trip non-stop, or refuel at Flint, Michigan.

28. ICEX; a trade name for semi-liquid substance with a mucus appearance that is applied to the icing equipment to lessen the adhesion of ice on these surfaces.

Chapter Ten

29. A three-dimensional triangle lying on its side; when balanced properly is susceptible to the slightest breeze. Because of its shape, unlike a windsock; it will point into the wind and toward the direction of landing.

30. He was the ventriloquist, Paul Winchell.

31. Actor Robert Cummings. He had also been a flight instructor for the military in WW II. It has been reported, he has civilian flight instructor certificate number one.

Chapter Eleven

32. The "T" tail design was fashioned to resemble those used on many jet airliners, and is mostly for aesthetics. The stabilator is located high off the ground; preflight of the tail section is performed from the top of a tall ladder. The other method, have someone hold the tail on the ground while the pilot performed his inspection. Both methods are an inconvenience.

33. This was started at many of the major hubs in the country; New York, Boston etc. Encompassing a large amount of restricted airspace around each hub, starting from the ground over each

facility and extending vertically and horizontally around that airport; similar to an inverted wedding cake. This was an effort to discourage training and leisure traffic from busy airports.

34. Before starting his new assignment, the Lieutenant and I had one last meeting; in the last three years, many of our graduates were among the top ten percent of the class at Pensacola.

Chapter Twelve

35. The pilot of a similar Aztec experienced a complete electrical failure after departing eastbound from Albany on a late winter evening. The starter on one of the engines remained engaged even after a successful start. The electrical drain was such; both alternators were unable to keep the electrical system operating. Without an electrical system, the pilot made an emergency landing on an unfinished bridge east of Albany that was covered with several inches of snow. The airplane was repaired and flown to Albany several days later. I checked the registration; consideration had been given for the purchase of this very aircraft, however, the blue color of 526 was more appealing.

Chapter Thirteen

36. A probe that senses airspeed reduction actuates an automatic gear extension override on the Arrow. A coating of ice will cause the sensor to react as though the airplane were flying at a slower speed.

37. The Pitot tube is part of the system measuring the speed of the airplane through the air. Equipped with an electric element, it is heated to prevent moisture from freezing and rendering it inoperative.

Chapter Fourteen

38. Tail dragger is the term used for any airplane equipped with a tail wheel.

39. The magnetic compass is just that; any thing electrical in the airplane will create a magnetic disturbance to some degree. A compass correction card is supplied for each airplane telling the pilot the expected error when the radios are on or off. Unexpected electrical problems can render the compass unreliable.

Chapter Fifteen

40. On multi-engine airplanes I have previously flown, the loss of one engine on takes off means an immediate abort. Transport category aircraft are required to accelerate to take off airspeed even after loosing an engine beyond the V1 critical speed.

41. Structural icing is associated with visible moisture and temperatures of zero degrees or slightly below. Hot air is piped from the engines to the leading edges of the wing and tail to melt the ice.

42. The New York Terminal Control Area is one of the largest and busiest in the country, controlling the traffic for three large airports; JFK, LaGuardia and Newark. To operate in this airspace requires an ATC clearance regardless of weather conditions.

43. Fred died. A victim of cancer.